The vineyard spreads beside the road
In repetition, point and line:
I sing, in this dry bright abode,
The praises of the native wine.
—*Yvor Winters*

WILDSAM PURSUITS

Places are endlessly complex: time, geography, culture and happenings layered with millions of stories. And often, one realizes that a place carries a specific heritage, a definitive pursuit that people build their lives around, a common trade or precious resource that might set the course for generations.

For Napa and Sonoma counties in California, this pursuit is wine.

Our deepest thanks goes to first responders and front-line health professionals in Napa and Sonoma counties, who dealt with fires and a pandemic while we were creating this book. Special thanks to Jullianne Ballou and the team at the University of California, Davis Shields Library Archives and Special Collections. Our research benefited from the insight of Jordan Michelman, Katherine Cole, Damon Wong, Anne Semans, Hardy Wallace, Andrew Mariani, Patrick Shabram, Dan Petroski, David Ahern and many others. Thanks to Angela Hardin and Richard McDaniel for easing the path to "Osprey Talks to Me One Day." Neil Alexander Walker wrote our Almanac piece on the Southern Pomo language.

WILDSAM FIELD GUIDES™

Copyright © 2020

All rights reserved. No portion of this
book may be reproduced in any form without
permission from the publisher.

Published in the United States
by Wildsam Field Guides, Austin, Texas.

ISBN 978-1-4671-9940-7

Illustrations by Liana Jegers

To find more field guides, please visit
www.wildsam.com

CONTENTS

*Discover the people and places
that tell the story of Napa and Sonoma*

ESSENTIALS	007

*Trusted intel and travel info about iconic places
and important topics*

ATLAS	015

*A guide to the key places of these counties:
curated favorites, cities and towns and a wineland itinerary*

ALMANAC	037

*Archival excerpts, timelines, clippings and
other historical musings*

PURSUIT	061

*A field guide to wine, with notes on tasting, production,
science, geography and the history of the endeavor*

INTERVIEWS	073

*Concise and meaningful one-way conversations
with locals of note*

STORIES	091

*Personal essays from writers with deep perspective
on Northern California's landscape and culture*

WINE DIRECTORY & INDEX	115

NOTES	122

FOLDOUT MAP	129

WELCOME

UP TOWARD NAPA SODA SPRINGS the roads get lonely. The valley floor, its tasting rooms and tourist vineyard bustle all fade in the rearview. Oaks up here seem just plain gnarlier, branches twisting up into dark fright wigs. The road dead-ends at a locked gate between worn stone columns. In the 1870s, this gate led to a palatial resort, built around the mineral waters that fizz up through Napa's soils.

Bowling greens. Exotic gardens. A rotunda where bands played quadrilles. The draw, then as now, was Northern California's promise of good living on a sublime landscape. But rugged tales played out behind the walls, too: feuds, fires and fading appeal. Now only ghostly shells stand amid dry woods. You might catch a glimpse from the road.

Napa Soda Springs lingered in mind as we traveled through Napa and Sonoma, its foggy wine country sister. In the right circumstances, life in these counties—more than 2,500 square miles combined, bigger than Delaware—can be idyllic. Kicked back with sun, sea breeze and a Napa cab or Sonoma pinot, the feeling is tangible: These valleys on either side of the Mayacamas Mountains, together, are *the* place that has it all figured out. But in truth life is tougher and more complicated, as always. As we worked on this book, fires ripped through Napa and Sonoma, menacing Calistoga, pushing Santa Rosa evacuations, damaging famed tourist destinations. The stress is acute, especially for folks in the fields and kitchens.

And recent disaster takes its place in a long human story here, as full of drama, tragedy and twists as any you'll find. Lonely Russians at Fort Ross. Indigenous cultures, resilient in the face of violent oppression. Fired-up rebels beneath a handmade Bear Flag. Chinese cellar-builders and immigrants from Southern Europe's back corners. Back-to-landers and would-be moguls.

The reality here is complex because the lure is so palpable, felt on any Highway 1 headland or Napa vineyard back road. Adversity aside, there's that notion that here we could get it right. And we need places like this, where the moment can be warm and the future enticing. Napa Soda Springs has been on the market of late, by the way. They're saying it could be a great opportunity. —The Editors

SELECTED CONTENT

008 *Planning*
009 *Geography and Traditions*
010 *Wine Destinations and Cultural Institutions*
011 *Scenic Drives and Public Lands*
012 *Film, Music and Books*
013 *Issues and Statistics*

ESSENTIALS

Trusted intel and traveler info about iconic culture, geography, traditions and entry points to Napa and Sonoma wine and landscape

ESSENTIALS

PLANNING

TRANSPORT

OFF-ROAD TRUCK
Bohemian Highway
Sonoma
bohohwy.com

PUBLIC TRANSIT
The Vine
Napa
vinetransit.com

ROAD BIKE
Napa River Velo
Napa
naparivervelo.com

LANDMARKS

BEAR FLAG MONUMENT
E Spain St, Sonoma Plaza
Throwback shrine to rebellion, short-lived California Republic.

CHARLES KRUG WINERY
2800 Main St, St Helena
Imposing 1861 testament to Napa wine's origins.

MEDIA

RADIO
KBBF 89.1 FM
Historic bilingual public station since 1973.

NEWSPAPER
Santa Rosa Press Democrat
The Pulitzer winner for heroic 2017 fire coverage.

CLIMATE

Variety rules. Rivers wind through cool, shady valleys not far from sunbaked, gnarly oaks. Sea breezes drift far inland through mountain gaps. Napa's sunshine builds mighty cabernets, and winter lows only flirt with freezing. In Sonoma, startling chill after torrid days heralds the sea, with coast-born fogs key to both mood and the land's fertility. [Spring is a choice time. Word to the wise.] Recent fires serve notice that all this beauty depends on an imperiled balance of sun, water and wind.

CALENDAR

JAN	Cabernet season
FEB	Sonoma Coast whale watching
MAR	Budbreak [wine growth cycle begins]
APR	Bodega Bay rockfish season opener
MAY	BottleRock music festival
JUN	Pacific Association indie baseball
JUL	Bohemian Grove conclave
AUG	Town & Country Fair
SEP	Peak grape harvest season
OCT	Napa Valley Latino Heritage Month
NOV	Nouveau season
DEC	Winemakers rack and barrel future wines

GEOGRAPHY

Notable terrain formations and where to find them.

OAK WOODLAND
Uncommon tree diversity, with grassy understories never disturbed by grazers. *Trione-Annadel State Park, near Santa Rosa*

CALIFORNIA CHAPARRAL
High scrub suited to Mediterranean climate. Key bird habitat. *Foote Botanical Preserve, Napa*

COASTAL PRAIRIE
Endangered wildflower troves meeting rocky Pacific headlands, with vital diversity. *Bohemia Ecological Preserve, Occidental*

TIDAL WETLANDS
Bayside survivors, encompassing sloughs and marshes, rich with life. *Napa River Bay Trail, American Canyon*

GEYSERS
Complex underground stirrings underlie a nexus of geothermal power. *Old Faithful Geyser of California, Calistoga*

PYGMY FOREST
Uncanny biome along tough seaside: old trees, mostly pine and cypress, only a few feet tall. *Salt Point State Park, Sonoma*

TRADITIONS

A fertile heritage of food, goods and skill goes far beyond wine.

Olive Oil	Olives thrive in this climate—Sonoma Valley's second-largest harvest. *The Olive Press, Napa*
Cork Bark	Harvested every decade, trees live 100-plus years. Napa is the trade's American center. *Portocork, Napa*
Architecture	Old West downtowns, Victorian piles, faux palazzi and modernist ecobuilding projects: wine country backdrops striking design. *Aperture Estate, Healdsburg*
Cheese	Immigrant heritage and modern artisan trends combine to produce one of America's great cheese cultures. *Vella Mezzo Secco, Sonoma*
Fruit	Orcharding began with Russian outposts in 1811. Sonoma champions the Gravenstein apple, and farm stands dot the roads. *Olympia's Orchard, Petaluma*

ESSENTIALS

WINE DESTINATIONS

Ten orientation points among the nearly limitless options.

NAPA

ASHES & DIAMONDS
Midcentury design vibes, bloody delicious wines

NICHELINI
Age-old family place, deep in lost hills

SCHRAMSBERG
Classic 1800s and 1960s history, sparkling gems

STONY HILL
Chardonnays that erase the bad ones

OUTLAND
Tasting room for three sharp indie wineries

SONOMA

SCRIBE
Beautiful, bright wines, glorious hacienda

COPPOLA
Huge and fun—jump in the pool

GUNDLACH BUNDSCHU
Six generations in, also a noted music venue

RIDGE
Refined and exacting since the '60s

HIRSCH
Revered coast vines, Healdsburg tasting room

CULTURAL INSTITUTIONS

ROBERT LOUIS STEVENSON MUSEUM
1490 Library Ln, St Helena
The Scottish author honeymooned in Napa, origin of 1883's *The Silverado Squatters* and this center of archives and memorabilia.

....

THE HESS COLLECTION
4411 Redwood Rd, Napa
Swiss magnate Donald Hess gathers blue-chip art world names: Motherwell, Stella, Rauschenberg, Bacon. Inquire in advance.

....

CALIFORNIA INDIAN MUSEUM AND CULTURAL CENTER
5250 Aero Dr, Santa Rosa
A rally point for language renewal, tribal history and sovereignty, craft and visual arts.

SCENIC DRIVES
AND PUBLIC LANDS

Backroad journeys and natural sites in two diverse counties.

BOHEMIAN HIGHWAY
Short drive, but you may never leave these California-dreamy hamlets and Russian River woods. Ravioli and a spritz at Negri's sounds right. *Sonoma County, Freestone to Monte Rio*

SAGE CANYON ROAD
Crank the Eagles and twist through tawny hills, past old-time wineries to a lonely county-line turnout atop the dam. *Napa County, Silverado Trail to Monticello Dam*

NAPA SOLANO RIDGE TRAIL
A rigorous 10-miler to clear heads and cleanse pores, reaching brand-new Suscol Headwaters Park and sweeping views. *Skyline Wilderness Park, Napa*

BODEGA HEAD TRAIL
Watch for whales and get that edge-of-the-world feeling amid crabbing opportunities and harbor seal encounters. Find your way to Portuguese Beach, Shell Beach, Duncan's Landing, other fave seaside spots. *Sonoma Coast State Park*

SANTA ROSA RURAL CEMETERY
White oaks grow around grave markers from the 1850s. Wildflowers [and, by legend, ghosts] abound across 17 acres. *1600 Franklin Ave, Santa Rosa*

BOTHE-NAPA VALLEY STATE PARK
A pretty mashup of chill and rugged, with woodsy hikes, rented yurts and cabins, and a pool, but also stirring climbs up Coyote Peak. *3810 St Helena Hwy, Calistoga*

WESTSIDE ROAD
Wineries dot a Russian River Valley [i.e., pinot-saturated] country road that takes you where you need to go [i.e., more wineries]. *Sonoma County, Healdsburg to Hilton*

ESSENTIALS

MEDIA

FILM
The Birds
Sideways
Thieves' Highway
The Earth Is Mine
Decanted
Somm
Wine Country
A Walk in the Clouds
Falcon Crest
American Graffiti
Bottle Shock
The Fog

MUSIC
The Limeliters
Time to Gather Seeds

Kate Wolf
Gold in California

Tom Waits
Mule Variations

David Luning
Just Drop on By

The Cramps
Live at Napa State Mental Hospital

BOOKS

▻ *The New California Wine* by Jon Bonné: On-the-road journalism, fierce scholarship and science combine to champion the most creative Cali wines.

▻ *The Girls* by Emma Cline: Celebrated fiction by a Sonoma native, imagining a link between a '60s Northern California kid and a Manson Family–like cult, masterfully evoking era and cultural texture.

▻ *Drop City* by T. Coraghessan Boyle: And as a companion piece, a novel based on the Diggers' Sonoma communal farm. Starry-eyed passages match the back-to-the-land impulse.

▻ *Napa: The Story of an American Eden* by James Conaway: Still sparking arguments after 30 years, a nonfiction tell-all of soap-opera intensity and girth worthy of a Michener tome. Worth it just for the Gallo brothers.

▻ *The House of Mondavi* by Julia Flynn Siler: A deeply reported examination of one family's wine saga traces the creation of modern Napa and some memorably juicy dynastic battles.

▻ *Already Dead* by Denis Johnson: The late laureate of lost Western souls sets a "California gothic" on the Sonoma Coast, along Highway 1.

ISSUES

Fire and Climate	Fire is elemental to California's landscape. But more severe climate extremes exacerbate conditions for destruction. Grape vines do act as firebreaks, often saving wineries, but the fate of everyday lives hinges on luck, wind and firefighters. **EXPERT**: *Steve Akre, Sonoma Valley Volunteer Firefighters Association*
Family Farms	Ancestral vineyards loom large in wine mystique. But costly permits often prohibit family-owned vineyards from opening on-site tasting rooms. Multigenerational farmers seek a "micro-winery ordinance" to survive in an increasingly corporate Napa Valley. **EXPERT**: *George O'Meara, president, Save the Family Farms*
Housing	A coveted region was already pricey before destructive fires further pressured supply. Both counties face labor shortages because blue-collar workers can't afford them. The remote-office trend and rumors of urban exodus make the market even more competitive. **EXPERT**: *Joelle Gallagher, Napa Housing Coalition*
The Market	Wine faces converging challenges, from grape oversupply to new-minted wisdom that "millennials don't drink wine." Competition and changing tastes do curb full-tilt price-boosting—possibly a 25-year growth spurt's end. But new styles and younger clienteles mean opportunity, too. **EXPERT**: *Rob McMillan, Silicon Valley Bank*

STATISTICS

34.6%	Hispanic population in Napa County, 2019
6,760	Latino-owned businesses in Sonoma County
110,700	Acres burned in 2017 Sonoma Complex wildfire
$937M	Estimated value, Napa County wine crop, 2019
96,000	Wine gallons lost to Russian River in 2020 Rodney Strong spill
$8,800	Screaming Eagle 1992 Cab Sauv bottle price [if found]

SELECTED CONTENT

016 BESTS

Food & Drink
Lodging
Outdoors
Shops
Artists & Makers
Events
Experts

024 CITIES & TOWNS

Napa, Somona, Healdsburg, Guerneville, Calistoga, St. Helena, Yountville, Santa Rosa, Petaluma and Sebastopol

030 ROAD TRIP

A five-day itinerary across wine country

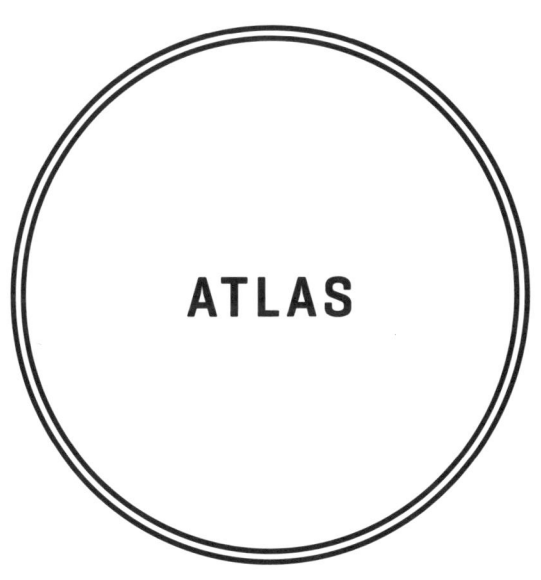

ATLAS

A guide to Napa and Sonoma's lands and places, including curated favorites, communities large and small, and a soulful journey into wine country's heart

ATLAS

BESTS

FOOD & DRINK

For winery recommendations, see pages 67-69.

AMERICAN CLASSIC
The French Laundry
6640 Washington St
Yountville
Thomas Keller's tasting-menu shrine. Book eons ahead [and invest] for the prix fixe.

MEXICAN
El Molino Central
11 Central Ave
Sonoma
Bighearted joint for enchiladas and tacos, on every short list for true masa.

POWER LUNCH
Mustards Grill
7399 St Helena Hwy
Napa
Brawny fare ["famous Mongolian pork chop"] for shop-talking winemakers.

ITALIAN MARKET
Genova Delicatessen
1550 Trancas St
Napa
One inhale and you know this place is the real deal. Supplying pasta, wine and deli to nonnas since '26.

FARM-TO-TABLE
The Girl & The Fig
110 W Spain St
Sonoma
Frenchified Sonoma: avocado toast to wild flounder meunière.

SANDWICHES
Contimo Provisions
950 Randolph St
Napa
That mortadella you've been questing for, plus coffee by favorite roaster Naysayer.

DIVE BAR
The Green Door
2955 Solano Ave
Napa
A locals' staple, more like the last stop of the night than the first. Maybe leave your car.

CIDER
Bardos
bardoscider.com
Sonoma
Crafted from rediscovered feral orchards. Seek and ye shall find.

TACO TRUCKS
Tacos Chavez [Napa]
Cabeza only.
Mercadito [Napa]
Noted vegan options.
Guerneville Taco Truck
Safeway lot.

FRENCH BISTRO
Bistro Jeanty
6510 Washington St
Yountville

The steak frites and cassoulet that wine country demands.

....

RED-SAUCE JOINT
Volpi's
124 Washington St
Petaluma

Century-old stronghold of accordion tarantellas and polenta.

....

FRIED CHICKEN
Ad Hoc
6475 Washington St
Yountville

Keller's crew lets its hair down for fried-chicken nights.

....

BURGER WITH FRIES
Compline
1300 1st St, #312
Napa

A wine bar, but Jammir Gray turns out one of the best.

....

BREAKFAST SANDWICH
The Model Bakery
1357 Main St
St Helena

House-made English muffins bearing morning-after cures.

BUTCHER
The Fatted Calf
Oxbow Public Market
Napa

Well-sourced cuts highlight a sparkling public market.

....

GERMAN
Brot
16218 Main St
Guerneville

Wursts and döner from Boon Hotel's Crista Luedtke, a G-Ville mainstay.

....

PUERTO RICAN
El Coqui
400 Mendocino Ave
Santa Rosa

A festive Tropicália surprise, slicing sought-after chuletas.

....

PIZZA
Tra Vigne Pizzeria
1016 Main St
St Helena

Back-pocket choice for wood-fired pies.

....

FAMILY DINNER
Farmstead
738 Main St
St Helena

Estate meats and a dreamy patio. Deviled eggs are deluxe.

DINER
Dierk's Parkside Cafe
404 Santa Rosa Ave
Santa Rosa

A big-breakfast standby, with a sprawling menu.

....

PASTRIES
Butter Cream Bakery
2297 Jefferson St
Napa

Deep doughnut game since the '40s.

....

OLD HAUNT
Old Main Street Saloon
153 N Main St
Sebastopol

A train runs around the ceiling. Just like you imagine.

....

SUSHI & IZAKAYA
Miminashi
821 Coombs St
Napa

Sashimi, ramen, tikified Spam and a legit mai tai.

....

BREWERY
Mad Fritz
393 La Fata
St Helena

Every beer from a unique barrel, gonzo faves like the Donkey and Thistle.

ATLAS

LODGING

WILD PACIFIC

Timber Cove
North of Jenner
timbercoveresort.com
Midcentury stunner on rugged headlands. Ansel Adams took epic surf shots here.

....

CURATIVE RETREAT

Indian Springs
Calistoga
indianspringscalistoga.com
Throwback Cali idyll of sparkling waters, classic cottages and lawn games.

....

RYOKAN

SingleThread
Healdsburg
singlethreadfarms.com
Japanese-inspired stay with lavish farm-driven food.

....

VINTAGE MOTEL

El Bonita
St Helena
elbonita.com
Nice retro spot, strategically nooked between town and vineyards.

BED-AND-BREAKFAST

Embrace Calistoga
Calistoga
embracecalistoga.com
A classic B&B situation with just the right amount of old-fashioned charm.

....

COUNTRY BOHEMIAN

Boon Hotel + Spa
Guerneville
boonhotels.com
Crisp design, free-booting river-and-redwoods vibes.

....

DOWNTOWN CLASSIC

Hotel La Rose
Santa Rosa
hotellarose.com
Stately gem in SR's Railroad Square—walk everywhere.

....

CLEANSING PLUNGE

Calistoga Motor Lodge and Spa
Calistoga
calistogamotorlodge.com
High-design pool life, mud baths, steam room and claw-foot tubs.

RETRO MOD

The Astro
Santa Rosa
theastro.com
Jetsons-esque motel reboot. Big love for its neighborhood.

....

PROVENCE X CALI

Auberge du Soleil
Napa
aubergeresorts.com
Just maybe the Napa you fantasize: suites, studios or "private maisons" in a South of France vein.

....

GREEN LUXURY

Bardessono
Yountville
bardessono.com
Village-like setup, rarefied eco-aims [and price, but hey].

....

AIRSTREAMS

AutoCamp
Russian River
Guerneville
autocamp.com
Fancy campers amid redwoods, a quick jaunt to town.

OUTDOORS

SURFBOARDS
Northern Light Surf Shop
Bodega Bay
northernlightsurf.com
Famed shaper Ed Barbera crafts boards in the red shed.

BOCCE
Crane Park
St Helena
cityofsthelena.org
Once flashpoint of interclub conflict. Now, peace prevails but seasonal league play is serious.

NAPA DAY HIKE
Oat Hill Mine
Calistoga
napaoutdoors.org
Eight rugged miles of forest, chaparral and rural ruins.

SONOMA DAY HIKE
East Ridge Trail
Armstrong Redwoods State Natural Reserve
About 6 miles with plenty of climbs, trees and views.

REDWOODS
Harold Richardson Redwoods Reserve
savetheredwoods.org
Once-secret, near-mythic Sonoma ancient tree stash.

RUNNING GEAR
Healdsburg Running Company
Healdsburg
healdsburgrunningcompany.com
One of those rock-solid shops, nexus for runs and races.

KAYAKING
Napa Valley Paddle
Napa
napavalleypaddle.com
Rental craft, lessons and guided tours into wild wetlands close to town.

HOT AIR BALLOONS
Napa Valley Aloft
Yountville
nvaloft.com
The venerable outfit, with multiple launch sites and flight plans.

BEACH
Bodega Dunes
Sonoma Coast State Park
parks.ca.gov
Seaside campground with amenities. Angle for Site 65.

SAILING
Bodega Bay Sailing
bodegabaysailing.com
Tour sea lion playgrounds and offshore rocks.

HORSEBACK
Triple Creek Horse Outfit
Glen Ellen
triplecreekhorseoutfit.com
Saddle up for rides through vineyards and woods in Jack London State Park.

SUPERCAR
Club Sportiva
San Francisco
clubsportiva.com
A Maserati Gran-Tourismo in wine country? Let's make that happen.

ATLAS

SHOPS

JEWELRY
Gallery Lulo
303 Center St
Healdsburg
Modernist statement pieces alongside painting and sculpture.

....

DESIGN
Erin Martin
1350 Main St
St Helena
Outré art meets stylish décor. When "over the top" is your starting point.

....

KITCHENWARE
Shackford's
1350 Main St
Napa
All the tools, plus knife sharpening and in-house kitchen.

....

AG SUPPLIES
Western Farm Center
21 W 7th St
Santa Rosa
Hardworking stockist of feed, chickens, beekeeping gear, etc.

BOUTIQUE
Scout West County
418 Healdsburg Ave
Healdsburg
Great eye for artisan brands across clothes, home, paper, beauty.

....

EMPORIUM
The CIA at Copia
500 1st St
Napa
As much art and culture center as culinary goods trove.

....

CHEESE
Oxbow Wine & Cheese
610 1st St
Napa
Sprawling *fromage* array in Napa's lovely public market.

....

GENERAL STORE
Dry Creek General Store
3495 Dry Creek Rd
Healdsburg
Dating to the 1880s, now sells luscious deli and produce.

HARDWARE
Steve's Hardware
1370 Main St
St Helena
A real-deal Ace. Deep local roots. Power tools.

....

FARM STAND
Big Ranch Farms
2046 Big Ranch Rd
Napa
Fresh-plus produce. Owners usually on hand for questions.

....

VINTAGE
Opera House Collective
145 Kentucky St
Petaluma
Great hunting by a trio of like-minded vendors.

....

BOOKSTORES
Bookmine
Napa, St Helena
Copperfield's
Petaluma, Calistoga
Readers' Books
Sonoma
Treehorn
Santa Rosa

ARTISTS & MAKERS

COOPER

Seguin Moreau
Napa
seguinmoreaunapa.com
A seasoned wine barrel maker, fire-toasting French oak and other woods.

....

LETTERPRESS

Shipwright & Co.
Napa
shipwrightandco.com
Custom designs, century-old gear and a fine eye for type.

....

CREATIVE COMPOUNDS

Carter & Co.
St Helena
carterandco.com
Townie shop for beautiful stoneware; remote ranch for high-minded arts talk.

....

LANDSCAPE PAINTER

Richard McDaniel
Santa Rosa
richardmcdaniel.com
Documenting Russian River scenes en plein air: bursts of new grass after fires.

PERFUME

Godseye
Santa Rosa
godseyeoils.com
Scents imbued with Cali-style groove.

....

TIENDITA

Alma's Oil Cloth and Chucherias
Healdsburg
almasoilclothandchucherias.com
Vivid handmade Mexican paper flowers, oilcloths and altars.

....

ABSTRACT ART

Mikey Kelly
Napa
mikeykelley.com
Paintings, drawings, sculptures with geometric precision.

....

LEATHERWORKER

Lu Comora
Santa Rosa
balaschool.com
Handbag boutique Bohlux's founder teaches Old World techniques.

BOTTLE DESIGN

Tina Carpenter
Napa
carpenter-creative.com
Stately labels and brand design evoking a heavyweight cabernet vibe.

....

FURNITURE

Furniture Marolles
Napa
furnituremarolles.com
A daughter-father team revives 1960s French wooden chair design.

....

POETS LAUREATE

Phyllis Meshulam
Sonoma County
phyllismpoet.com
A stalwart advocate for grassroots verse. Her own lines are sharp-eyed.

Jeremy Benson
Napa County
jerbenson.org
Hands-in-the-dirt voice: farmer, writer and community presence.

ATLAS

EVENTS

MUSIC FESTIVAL

Huichica
Sonoma, June
huichica.com
Indie tunes waft through the vines.

....

TALENT SHOW

Monte Rio Variety Show
Monte Rio, July
monterioshow.wordpress.com
Secretive Bohemian Grove's public shindig. Big names from Bing Crosby to Asleep at the Wheel.

....

STREET FESTIVAL

Porchfest
Napa, July
napaporchfest.org
Local bands set up outdoors for a communal wander.

....

BOOK FESTIVAL

Sonoma Valley Authors Festival
Sonoma, August
svauthorsfest.org
Marquee writers and local authors gather.

FOOD FESTIVALS

California Artisan Cheese Festival
Santa Rosa, March
artisancheesefestival.com
Educational [and, uh, delicious] showcase of NorCal cheese glory.

———

Butter & Egg Days
Petaluma, April
petalumadowntown.com
"Egg Basket of the World" shows off ag town bona fides.

....

SOCCER

Napa Valley 1839 FC
Napa, Spring–Summer
napavalley1839.com
Local semi-pros take on regional rivals in a grassroots league.

....

RODEO

Bay Area Rodeo
Duncan Mills,
September
bayarearodeo.com
A top LGBTQ rodeo. Full events slate: chute dogging, steer deco, etc.

POWWOW

Suscol Intertribal Powwow
Napa, October
suscolcouncil.org
Drums, dance, traditional arts meet-up for Indigenous culture.

....

HERITAGE

Festa Italiana
St Helena, July
vsattui.com
A toast to Italian and Swiss-Italian roots. Wild boar, tiramisu.

....

CINEMA

Sonoma International Film Festival
Sonoma, March
sonomafilmfest.org
Noted for high quality and diversity commitments.

....

ARTISANS

Napa Makes
Napa, June
napamakes.org
Craft and goods happening draws Bay Area creators.

EXPERTS

WINE CRITIC
Esther Mobley
San Francisco Chronicle
Authoritative reporting with an eye for hard news and true talent.

COMMUNITY ACTION
Rebuild NorthBay
rebuildnorthbay.org
A multidimensional effort to stoke fire recovery at the grassroots, from forestry to housing.

INTERIOR DESIGN
Bette Abbott
betteabbott.com
The gleaming modern farmhouse in your mind's eye can get some help from a seasoned pro.

WATER WITCH
Marc Mondavi
ckmondavi.com
Wine clan patriarch finds hidden waters using secret powers. True story.

COASTAL BIOLOGY
Jacqueline Sones
University of California, Davis
Focused on Bodega Bay ecology and climate-change impacts.

PUBLIC ART
Gordon Huether
gordonhuether.com
Grand-scale works across the country, studio here. Look for the giant hand.

LANDSCAPE ARCHITECTURE
Roche + Roche
rocheandroche.com
Wife-and-husband firm applying regional smarts to home, estate and vineyard grounds.

ASIAN AMERICAN HISTORY
Cecilia Tsu
University of California, Davis
Studying Asian migration in the West, key to both counties' stories.

BACKYARD VINEYARDS
David Layland
ucanr.edu
A University of California master gardener has lived the DIY trials.

LINGUISTICS
Neil Alexander Walker
Western Institute for Endangered Language Documentation
Cataloging Southern Pomo grammar, key for language revival.

CANNABIS
Elise McDonough
elisemcdonough.com
Santa Rosa edibles ace, author of *Bong Appetit* and *High Times*' cookbook.

IMMIGRATION
Madeline Hernandez
Immigration Institute of the Bay Area
Century-old outfit offering legal counsel to new Americans.

ATLAS

CITIES & TOWNS

These counties' settlements give you urbane bustle or back roads country charm. Here, ten communities and the places that make them hum.

NAPA

Used to be when folks said "Napa" they meant any part of Napa Valley except Napa, the town. But creative young blood and Bay Area money have coalesced. [Sometimes provoking a bit of local chagrin.] NAPA FARMERS MARKET provides Alice Waters—level plenty, while downtown neighbors give fresh perspective on the wine scene: bars CADET and COMPLINE and the OUTLAND tasting room. To see the real town, look beyond some of the new glitz to deep history, like the Chinatown that once stood at the Third Street Bridge. Tour the Tulocay Cemetery for graves marking Napa's earliest vintners, immigrants and founders. Tucked-away surprises include campy retiree favorite TRANCAS STEAKHOUSE [raucous karaoke] or sweet Il Posto Trattoria, a beloved Italian spot right off the side of Highway 29.

LUNCH STOP	
Gotts	POPULATION: 78,373
Burgers and shakes get ultra-luxe treatment	COFFEE: Naysayer, Ritual
	BEST DAY OF THE YEAR: Wild mustard bloom, January

SONOMA

Few West Coast cities radiate history like Sonoma. Seven flags fly on the plaza, tracking colonial moves from Sir Francis Drake [England, 1579] through Russian, Spanish, Mexican and American empires. Mission San Francisco Solano sits opposite the BEAR FLAG MONUMENT, site of roughshod rebellion that birthed California. [For a glimpse of the darker side of colonial times here, see the list of people buried in the mission compound.] Today's town, though, is timeless Cali chill. G's General Store serves expert retail in a miniature department store. READERS' BOOKS is the cultural anchor; MURPHY'S IRISH PUB, reputedly, is where deals go down. Ease in with a cocktail at STARLING, then wander.

LOCAL WRITER	
Andy Weinberger	POPULATION: 11,300
Readers' owner pens moody, charming mystery novels	COFFEE: Basque Boulangerie Café
	BEST DAY OF THE YEAR: Huichica Music Festival, June

HEALDSBURG

In a way, Healdsburg is all about efficiency. If you can't make it to any other part of Sonoma, the streets around this balmy town's central plaza bundle all good things, with fleets of tasting rooms, gourmet shops and galleries. Cult-famed coastal vineyard HIRSCH has its embassy here, for example, a key stop for decoding California wine's avant-garde. [Near town, HOUSE OF FLOWERS showcases erudite, acclaimed coastal wines.] Journeyman Meat Co. is the high-craft, Italian-inflected butcher around here, and NOBLE FOLK's "ice cream and pie bar" setup is a concept that deserves to go global. For true throwback curio, the HAND FAN MUSEUM is just what it says, a textured collection testifying to *deep* curatorial focus.

GALLERY STOP	POPULATION: 12,086
Erickson Fine Art	COFFEE: Plank
A venerable presence, NorCal artists a focus	BEST DAY OF THE YEAR: Healdsburg Jazz Festival, June

GUERNEVILLE

Of yore a logging burg called Stumptown, Guerneville found new destiny with its first known gay bar in 1958. By the '70s, an open-minded rep made this laid-back river community an LGBTQ+ vacation dream. Folks walk the streets in bikinis or leather chaps [especially for the annual LAZY BEAR WEEKEND] and the river is truly a judgment-free zone. Stay at 15-acre Dawn Ranch and hit the river at JOHNSON'S BEACH, or rent a canoe from Burke's to find silence along many stretches. Armstrong Redwoods State Natural Reserve holds a grove of the giant trees, including many over 1,000 years old. On the Old West–ish Main Street, find the classic gay dive RAINBOW CATTLE COMPANY—and/or hit historic Guerneville Bank Club for homemade ice cream.

VINTAGE SPOT	POPULATION: 4,808
Pat's International	COFFEE: Higher Ground
A diner since 1940, with ancient timber gear to prove it	BEST DAY OF THE YEAR: Pride Parade, June

CALISTOGA

Vintage hustler Sam Brannan vowed to make these hot springs the Saratoga of California, but it came out "the Calistoga of Sarafornia." Health-seekers still decompress here, and the mere sight of lush lawns and bijou cottages at **INDIAN SPRINGS** serves as therapy. Dr. Wilkinson's Backyard Resort & Mineral Springs offers a spiffed-up 1950s take on the mud-bath vibe. **COPPERFIELD'S BOOKS**' local branch and Blackbird's artisan homewares suit laid-back moods, as does a leisurely dinner at **EVANGELINE**, noted for fried chicken. The wine world takes an exhale, too. **TANK GARAGE WINERY** crushes lesser-known grapes into delirious one-off wines served out of an old gas station, with '80s power ballads blasting. Napa's far end, in every sense.

ART STOP	POPULATION: 5,246
Villa Ca'Toga	COFFEE: Cafe San Marco
Italian muralist Carlo Marchiori's rococo retreat	BEST DAY OF THE YEAR: Lighted Tractor Parade, December

ST. HELENA

Napa Valley's original economic engine, St. Helena abounds with vintage big names—**CHARLES KRUG** founded Napa's first commercial winery here in 1861, still an iconic anchor. Today, wine-wise, St. Helena is less about undercover gems than quintessential tours along Highway 29. Definite stops: **HALL**'s lavish modern art collection, **DEL DOTTO**'s decadent wine caves, Beringer's Rhine House, dating to 1884. In town, **CAMEO CINEMA** is the platonic-ideal indie movie house. Public tours and cooking classes inspire future kitchen exploits at the Culinary Institute of America's landmark 19th-century campus. The cash-only Napa Valley Olive Oil Company, founded 1931, stocks an old white barn floor to ceiling with gourmet goods. **MOORE CREEK PARK** refreshes with a network of trails and diverse ruggedness.

SHOP STOP	POPULATION: 6,081
La Luna Market and Taqueria	COFFEE: The Station
A Rutherford-area go-to for sundries, burritos, etc.	BEST DAY OF THE YEAR: Hometown Harvest Festival, October

YOUNTVILLE

Yountville jam-packs so many wine country indulgences into one mile, it's like Napa in a capsule. Anchoring the rep is **THE FRENCH LAUNDRY**, chef Thomas Keller's daily experiment in flavor intensity. [The late Anthony Bourdain: "the best restaurant in the world, period."] The prix fixe, costing hundreds of dollars, books up months out, but you can wander FL's culinary gardens for free, or visit allied **BOUCHON BISTRO** or fried-chicken spinoff **AD HOC**. Washington Street's tasting rooms offer refuge between 5 p.m. winery closures and 7:45 dinner tables: Try Girard, Somerston, Jessup, Stewart or Priest Ranch. Or ditch that scene entirely for pool and beer at locals-only dive **PANCHA'S**. And if you don't need tables, let alone waits for tables, Tacos Garcia never disappoints.

CULTURE STOP	POPULATION: 2,948 COFFEE: Ottimo
Napa Valley Museum *Fine art, history and pop culture—inflected exhibits*	BEST DAY OF THE YEAR: Washington Street Christmas lighting, November

SANTA ROSA

Santa Rosa is more workhorse than show pony: a hub city with stalwart agricultural roots and sleepy historic neighborhoods, all skewered by a badly planned highway. Today, you can feel revival percolating at places like **THE SPINSTER SISTERS**, a homey, farm-driven restaurant with a deep community connection to the striving South of A Street Arts District. [The restaurant is linked to **THE ASTRO**, a retro-mod hotel.] Tiny, bright shop Miracle Plum curates a fascinating wine list—emphasis on natural—alongside smart cookbooks, beauty and pantry wares. Russian River Brewing Company is the region's big name in beer, but **FOGBELT**'s wild IPA lineup needs a look, too. And keep it under your hat: **TING HAU** might just have the best wonton soup in California.

HAPPY HOUR	POPULATION: 177,132
Stark's Steak & Seafood *A classic red-booth joint is the reigning champ*	COFFEE: Flying Goat BEST DAY OF THE YEAR: National Heirloom Exposition, September

PETALUMA

You feel Petaluma's Old West roots as you stroll Water Street Promenade after a gin and tonic at classic dive HIDEAWAY or a pint at Volpi's, an Italian stallion of a restaurants that's been pouring since Prohibition days. Wander the Livestock Auction Yard for an agricultural crash course, plus a stellar Chicago dog from ROY'S. Stay at '20s-era HOTEL PETALUMA for low-key history. Nearby, Ernie's Tin Bar is an age-old locals' hang with a most welcome cellphone ban. THE WASHOE HOUSE has served as a watering hole since 1859, with a Cali-rare Civil War mythos to match. The "'Shoe" can serve as a takeoff point for a Pepper Road jaunt to Tomales Bay's oystering grounds.

FASHION STOP

Custom Costumes
*Outfitting Petaluma's many
Burning Man devotees*

POPULATION: 62,361
COFFEE: Acre Coffee
BEST DAY OF THE YEAR:
Rivertown Revival, July

SEBASTOPOL

Local, seasonal fare is big in Sebastopol, from the casual FARMER'S WIFE to the seafood-oriented Handline; the Barlow neighborhood is a nexus, including CROOKED GOAT BREWING and Blue Ridge Kitchen. Copperfield's Books has a beautiful location here, but do be sure to hit Second Chances to deep-dive for rare titles. Street artists Patrick Amiot and Brigitte Laurent have turned otherwise-humble FLORENCE AVENUE into an oddball promenade of sculptures fashioned from recycled flotsam. Go cider tasting at HORSE & PLOW, enjoy everyone's favorite ice cream at Screamin' Mimi's, and most definitely end your evening at OLD MAIN STREET SALOON, where you'll find classic booths, etched mirrors and locals who will let you in on the next round of pool.

OUTDOORS ROUTE

Joe Rodota Trail
*Cycle all the way
to Santa Rosa*

POPULATION: 7,714
COFFEE: Taylor Lane Organic Coffee
BEST DAY OF THE YEAR:
After the first rain

ATLAS

ROAD TRIP

For a wine country odyssey of landscapes, flavors, culture and history, start this ramble in the city, end at the sea.

DAY 1	**THE YOUNTVILLE RIDE** For a vibrant Napa starter course, mount up and roll to a village of near-surreal niceness.

To see real Napa at its most vivid, hop on two wheels. The NAPA VALLEY VINE TRAIL tours 12.5 paved miles through the city of Napa's working-class roots, into the tumble of verdant vineyards that line Highway 29 until reaching Yountville's luxe center. Rent rides from NAPA VALLEY BIKE TOURS in downtown Napa, then cruise a couple blocks to La Esperanza Tacos for exceptional handmade street food. Just a block away, the Vine Trail picks up next to ST. CLAIR BROWN WINERY & BREWERY, a handy early hydration stop and rare crossover: Elaine St. Clair stakes a claim as the nation's only woman working as both winemaker and brewmaster. Pedal alongside the tracks of industrial Napa, eyes peeled for murals. The trail straightens out at the scenic Oak Knoll section, where wine country's bucolic fantasy quickly percolates into the small-town reality. To your right, iconic wineries [Ashes & Diamonds, Trefethen] dot Highway 29; to your left, rows of vines serrate the valley floor. Pull off at ELYSE WINERY, a disarming setting for small-production zins and cabs from serious heritage vineyards. As the oak-shaded route bends into Yountville, pass the FRENCH LAUNDRY GARDENS, and wind up on WASHINGTON STREET, Yountville's epicenter of the good life. Stop at Jean-Charles Boisset's rococo ATELIER FINE FOODS for outrageous luxuries [caviar, foie gras], Bouchon Bakery for coveted macarons and a Restoration Hardware agog with chandeliers. Put your name in at CICCIO [no reservations], Yountville's groovy Italian charmer. Its repurposed market building boasts vintage Italian movie posters and handwritten butcher paper menus for a festive, unpretentious evening. Drink a negroni while you wait on Neapolitan pizza and crispy-skinned whole branzino. Too late to bike back? No problem—for a $20 fee, return your bike to Napa Valley Bike Tours' Yountville outpost, then call for your chariot [which may just be an Uber but could well feel like a chariot by now].

Napa's cycling heritage rolls deep. The Eagle Cycling Club debuted in press reports from 1897 and thrived through about 1914, organizing social dances, "club runs" and races. The club was revived around 1970. eaglecyclingclub.org

ATLAS

THE CARNEROS POINT-TO-POINT
Foggy bay breezes create a cooler climate perfect for pinot and chardonnay—and a welcome break from Napa Valley's spicier heat.

[For a satisfying arc, head west to east from the Sonoma County side.]

HIGHWAY 121
Explore CORNERSTONE SONOMA, where *Sunset* magazine's Test Gardens grow amid boutiques and tasting rooms. Angelo's Wine Country Deli [spot the rooftop cow] can supply a classic sandwich.

....

HIGHWAY 12 TO DENMARK STREET
Eastbound on 12, take increasingly bucolic turns to find a double-whammy of winery neighbors. Tastemaking SCRIBE WINERY serves farm-to-table snacks and terroir explorations at its sublime hacienda, a 19th-century estate once left to ruin [and turkey farming], now an idyll in the breezes of the Petaluma Gap. Next door, GUNDLACH BUNDSCHU WINERY, the oldest continuously family-owned winery in California, provides a perfectly unfussy experience on lush, sprawling grounds.

....

HIGHWAY 12 AND FREMONT DRIVE
Sop it all up with a crucial second lunch at LOU'S LUNCHEONETTE, a gourmet Southern roadside diner, before jumping back on the 12...wait, doesn't that hill over there, on the north side, look oddly familiar? It's Bliss, the site of Windows XP's ubiquitous boot-up screen, cited as the most viewed image in the world. [Sadly, new vines will bust your 1:1 re-creation attempts.]

....

HIGHWAY 12 AND DUHIG ROAD
Cross the Napa County line to find agrarian-chic HUDSON RANCH AND VINEYARDS: hikes through plush farmlands and wine picnics. Nearby, browse the di Rosa Center for Contemporary Art, a collection and sculpture garden featuring modern Northern Californian artists.

....

HIGHWAY 12 AND LOS CARNEROS
Land at CARNEROS RESORT & SPA for a dose of choose-your-own-unwind, from booking a pricey hilltop poolside cabana rental to a simple hangout by the fireplace at the outdoor pavilion for a post-road cocktail [your call]. Live music. Bocce. All things good and true.

| DAY 3 | **LARKMEAD: WINE PAST, WINE FUTURE**
 Head north toward Calistoga to find an insightful crossroads of old-time wine lore and future-focused innovation. |

Dating to 1895, Larkmead links to some of the industry's most significant names. And somehow, too, you can catch what's next here. "Napa wine goes back to the gold rush," says Dan Petroski, Larkmead's winemaker. "Immigrant culture, coming to America, setting out to find gold in those hills, instead creating California wine country." Petroski is a latter-day pilgrim: a 47-year-old former magazine pro self-remade into an acclaimed winemaker. He maintains a sharp eye for story, noting that Larry Solari, who bought Larkmead in 1948, was so pivotal to early California wine that jug-wine kings Ernest and Julio Gallo carried his casket. His Larkmead wines often nod to history. "Dr. Olmo," a structured cabernet sauvignon, pays tribute to Harold Olmo, "the Indiana Jones of grape-growing," as Petroski says. "He went to Afghanistan to learn about the origins of grape vines." Olmo conducted key research at Larkmead. Fittingly, today Petroski conducts salons on climate change and planting varieties suited to a transformed future. "Timing is everything," the winemaker says. "Varieties we're planting in 2020 were also planted at Larkmead in the '30s. It goes back to understanding what grows here."

ATLAS

EXPLORING OLIVET ROAD
Four wineries offer diverse entry points into the world-class Russian River Valley grape-growing region.

DELOACH VINEYARDS   *1791 Olivet Rd*

Founded by fireman Cecil DeLoach in 1975, this winery helped create the Russian River Valley American Viticultural Area, now one of the nation's brand-name wine territories. Pinots soar, as do dry riesling and beautiful gardens [and goats!].

....

HARVEST MOON   *2192 Olivet Rd*

Winemaker Randy Pitts is known for zins, but also makes beautiful dessert wines from late-harvest gewürztraminer. The down-home estate hits hospitality high notes while remaining amiable—a family-friendly, drinks-by-the-pool feel. Yes, the name is a Neil Young callout.

....

HOOK & LADDER   *2134 Olivet Rd*

The grandson of Cecil DeLoach helms this winery, producing from estate-grown fruit. Go for the chardonnay, stay for the fire department memorabilia.

....

IRON HORSE VINEYARDS   *9786 Ross Station Rd*

[*Olivet to the Guerneville Rd, 116 to Ross Station: 12 minutes*] Iron Horse began as a pinot house but is now renowned for sparkling wines, served at the White House for six administrations. [Reagan and Gorbachev toasted with Iron Horse.] CEO Joy Sterling is a political activist and industry force and the hilltop tasting room is not to be missed. Finish the day with handmade pasta at Canneti Roadhouse in Forestville.

> *Iron Horse and DeLoach are both key operations in the Green Valley AVA [American Viticultural Area, a federal designation]. Defining an AVA is complex. Wine observers have criticized some Northern California AVAs for being too broad. [Sonoma Coast AVA, for example, sprawls to some 500,000 acres.] With just 3,600 acres planted in grapes, Green Valley is one of the more particular regions, noted for specific soils and a climate cooler than neighboring areas.*

| DAY 5 | **THE COASTAL CLEANSE**
Time for a purifying wander out of doors, plus a detour to striking views of wild Pacific landscape and culture. |

The drive to the POMO CANYON ENVIRONMENTAL CAMPGROUND is a voyage in itself, best before the fog lifts off the Russian River. Stop in historic Duncans Mills for coffee from GOLD COAST BAKERY. The day's hike starts in ancient redwoods, on an ancestral trading route of the Coast Miwok and Pomo peoples, crossing many microclimates before reaching the Pacific. The redwoods and Douglas fir thin out to tanoak and bay, winnowing to shrub brush as you crest the hills. Sword ferns and trillium settle into buttercups and Queen Anne's lace. Take in the river before descending to the sea and sightlines all the way to Point Reyes southward, Goat Rock to the north. Back on wheels, cliff-hugging Highway 1 is the path to TIMBER COVE, a mid-century hotel slung on a jaw-loosening coastal rise. For an espresso shot to the spirit, look up 93 feet to the spire of the BUFANO PEACE STATUE MONUMENT by 20th-century San Francisco artist Beniamino Bufano. Also known as *The Expanding Universe*, the obelisk constitutes California's second-smallest state park. And with its images evoking cosmic and earthly harmony, it reminds us what the journey is for.

SELECTED CONTENT

038	*Vintage Napa boosterism*
039	*The Bear Flag Revolt*
041	*Winemakers of Note*
042	*Russian River Poets*
043	*Bohemian Grove*
045	*Historic bottles*
046	*Communes &* Falcon Crest
047	*Southern Pomo lexicon*
048	*Cesar Chavez & John Grider*
049	*The Sea Ranch*
050	*The French Laundry*
052	*Prohibition*
053	*Russian colony*
054	*Inglenook timeline*
057	*Hitchcock's* The Birds
059	*Jack London*

MORE THAN 30 ENTRIES ↦

ALMANAC

*A deep dive into the cultural heritage of
Napa and Sonoma through news clippings, timelines,
letters and other historical hearsay*

"OUR VALLEY HOME."

St. Helena Star
October 9, 1874

Poets have praised and travelers belauded in exultant strains the beauties found in various valleys in foreign climes. ... Place them side by side with our own sweet vale, yet unknown in song or poetic story, and we firmly believe that she would win the victor's crown in a contest for

SUPREMACY OF BEAUTY.

... But no Mediterranean dreaminess hovers around Napa's homes. It is filled with an intelligent,

THRIFTY, ENERGETIC RACE.

With the loveliness of Cashmere's noted valley it combines in its people the Grecian energy and the Roman will. The races that have sought out and settled themselves within the rims of those lofty mountains do not mean to rest satisfied with the natural gifts of

SOIL AND CLIMATE

They find here. ... Already, after only a score of years' reclamation from the wilderness and savagery, what do we behold? The screech of the locomotive, [the cry of commerce] is heard on our mountain tops, the

VINE AND THE FIG TREE

mark the settler's domicile. The wheat field and the vineyard spread out in beautiful contrast on the landscape ... Curative waters are found, and their localities beautified and the afflicted invited to come, and be cured. ... Not only the soil, but the impalpable air ministers to our wealth and produces the

THE ABUNDANT GRAPE:

... Neither blight nor failure visit our valley, and plenty, peace, prosperity and the highest civilization seems the future lot of the favored inhabitants of the peerless valley of Napa.

The region's wine literature is rich in claim-staking and boosterism. In the middle 20th century, viticulture researcher **HAROLD OLMO** *wrote: "We have long passed the stage ... in the wine industry when it was necessary to imitate or copy the elders ... The improvement and naming of our own varieties can lead to new and distinguished wines with the birthright of California. Let us become the imitated and not the imitators."*

THE BEAR FLAG REVOLT

PROCLAMATION

To all persons, citizens of Sonoma, requesting them to remain at peace, and to follow their rightful occupations without fear of molestation. The commander-in-chief of the troops assembled at the fortress of Sonoma, gives his inviolable pledge to all persons in California, not found under arms, that they shall not be disturbed in their persons, their property or social relations, one to another, by men under his command. He also solemnly declares his object to be, first, to defend himself and companions in arms, who were invited to this country by a promise of lands on which to settle themselves and families; who were also promised a republican government … who, instead of being allowed to participate in, or being protected by a republican government, were oppressed by a military despotism; who were even threatened by proclamation from the chief officer of the aforesaid despotism, with extermination if they would not depart out of the country. … [W]e were to be driven through deserts inhabited by hostile Indians to certain destruction. To overthrow a government which has seized upon the property of the Mission for its individual aggrandizement; which has ruined and shamefully oppressed the laboring people of California by their enormous exactions on goods imported into this country, is the *determined* purpose of the brave men who are associated under his command. … He further declares, that he believes that a government to be prosperous and happyfying in its tendency, must originate with its people, who are friendly to its existence; that its citizens are its guardians; its officers and its servants, and its glory, their reward.
—WILLIAM B. IDE, *Commander, Head Quarters, Sonoma, June 15, 1846*

Ide's proclamation came after a small contingent of armed Americans seized the Mexican barracks and raised a crude flag declaring a "CALIFORNIA REPUBLIC" *over Sonoma Plaza. [The version above appeared in* The Oregon Spectator; *another shortly appeared in Honolulu's* The Polynesian.] *Lore suggests Spanish-speaking onlookers mistook the heraldic bear for a pig. Both revolt and republic proved short-lived. By July, U.S. Army and Navy forces asserted control over California, replacing the Bear Flag with the Stars and Stripes.*

PHYLLOXERA

Native to the Eastern U.S., this vine-destroying aphid made its way to California via steamship. Below, an excerpt from an 1887 state ag report.

The spread of this insect has been far more rapid during the past season—favored by drought as it has been—than ever before. Abundant new spots have become manifest, and several new districts have been added to the quarantine list. ... I have found the winged insects common throughout the months of June, July, August, and September, giving them a long season in which to increase the infected territory. Few of our vineyardists appreciate the fact that the progression governing the increase of this pest is one of geometrical ratio—not an additive one; and though it may be several years before the presence of a few insects become evident in the vineyard, from that time on the spread is alarming ... the giving way of a few acres, or even a few hundred vines, means the loss of all within a limited number of years.

COUNTERFEIT WINE

WILLIAM I. KOCH VS. RUDY KURNIAWAN
PLAINTIFF'S COMPLAINT FOR FRAUD

Before he turned 30, Rudy Kurniawan became the most prominent wine aficionado in Los Angeles, cutting a broad swath through high-end auctions and exclusive wine tastings. Coming out of nowhere, Kurniawan quickly became known as the youthful, ultra-wealthy foreigner who spent aggressively at wine auctions and bid up prices dramatically. ... [T]he *Los Angeles Times* wrote a glowing profile about him in December 2006, just after he turned 30, under the headline "$75,000 a case? He's buying." ... The Kurniawan story and lifestyle have begun to unravel. Twice in the last three years wine that Kurniawan was offering for sale at auction was pulled back in dramatic fashion by the auction house at the last minute ... because the wine was unquestionably counterfeit. —*September 10, 2009*

Rudy Kurniawan traced his wine enthusiasm to a bottle from Napa's Opus One. Convicted of audacious frauds, as of 2020 he is a federal prison inmate. He is said to possess savant-like wine-tasting talent.

WINEMAKERS OF NOTE

GENERAL MARIANO GUADALUPE VALLEJO Oft-rebellious governor of Mexican-ruled California turned Sonoma into his own dominion. Experimented with grape varieties in the 1830s and '40s.

AGOSTON HARASZTHY Hailed as the industry's father. Pest-born Hungarian noble, digger of Wisconsin wine cellars, gold rush migrant. He started Sonoma's Buena Vista in 1857 with Chinese labor, winemaker Charles Krug. Driven to Nicaragua by money woes, he vanished in '69.

CHARLES KRUG 1861: The bespectacled Prussian settles in St. Helena, sets up cider press, begins Napa's wine saga.

HEIDI BARRETT Among modern-day Napa players, she has a magnum résumé as creator of big-money Screaming Eagle, consultant to many, owner of her own La Sirena.

LOUIS MARTINI This bombastic Genoese [fast cars, pinkie rings] planted post-Prohibition zinfandel and cabernet sauvignon—far-seeing moves.

HELEN TURLEY A mentor to Barrett and others, Turley is noted for technical innovation and her own Marcassin Vineyard, a Sonoma benchmark.

ANDRÉ TCHELISTCHEFF Left for dead in Crimean snow during the Russian Civil War. Yugoslavia, Czechoslovakia, then France. Hired by Beaulieu in 1938, he redefined cab sauv and galvanized West Coast wine.

TEGAN PASSALACQUA Younger winemaker, older soul preserves historic vineyards, creates acclaimed bottles for Turley and his own Sandlands label.

WARREN WINIARSKI France never saw him coming: Stag's Leap cab sauv cleaned up at the famed 1976 Paris tasting. Still a key industry figure.

MARTHA MCCLELLAN Embodiment of elite current craft, she makes hard-to-find [and -afford] reds for Sloan, plus runs her own label, myriad projects.

ALMANAC

RUSSIAN RIVER POETS

A post-Beat verse movement sank woodsy Sonoma roots in the '60s and '70s. Notable names:

JEFFREY MILLER Doomy '70s wunderkind and cult figure, dead at 29

MARIANNE WARE Outspoken poetry scene ringleader, "passionate if prickly"

ANDREI CODRESCU Romanian-born sojourner in Monte Rio, NPR name and publisher

HUNCE VOELCKER Eccentric gay filmmaker and writer, author of 1973's *Sillycomb*

GAIL KING Monte Rio long-timer. "Some days / there is fog / that rolls / down the hills"

DAVID BROMIGE London-born, Canada-trained, quintessential NorCal transplant

PAT NOLAN Prolific poet, editor, translator, publisher of *Life of Crime* mag

TERRY EHRET Bay Area lifer, collective publisher-founder, ex–Sonoma County laureate

LUTHER BURBANK

"I firmly believe, from what I have seen, that this is the chosen spot of all this earth as far as Nature is concerned," botanist Luther Burbank wrote to his family in Massachusetts after he arrived in Santa Rosa in 1875. Burbank went on to spend 40 years building a reputation as a highly successful horticulturist. He developed more than 800 plant varieties, including the Shasta daisy, the plumcot and spineless cacti. After visiting him, Dutch botanist Hugo de Vries deemed Burbank a "plant wizard." Some of his efforts, among them plant hybrids found nowhere else, are now preserved at the Luther Burbank Experimental Farm in Sebastopol. However, as is sometimes the case with those who tinker with genes, there was a dark side to Burbank's thinking. That oft-quoted line about the "chosen spot of all this earth"? The next bit: "and the people are far better than the average." Burbank was a prominent eugenicist who saw sunny California as a fine place to cultivate a superior race of people. Despite this troubling legacy, his name adorns significant institutions in Santa Rosa, and the state of California celebrates Arbor Day on March 7—Luther Burbank's birthday.

BOHEMIAN GROVE

A bucolic Sonoma retreat hosts the San Francisco–based Bohemian Club's secretive annual gathering. All-male and confidential, the summer idyll has become a locus of conspiracy theory. In 1989, Spy *magazine writer Philip Weiss snuck in.*

During the day, idleness is encouraged. There are few rules, the most famous one being "Weaving Spiders Come Not Here"—in other words, don't do business in the Grove. The rule is widely ignored. Another, unwritten rule is that everyone drink—and that everyone drink all the time. This rule is strictly adhered to. "His method was to seize a large horse bucket, throw a hunk of ice into it, pour in several bottles of gin and a half a bottle of vermouth, and slosh it all around," goes one Grove recipe. The traditional 7:00 a.m. gin fizzes served in bed by camp valets set the pace. Throughout the skeet-shooting, the domino-playing and the museum talks, right up through the "afterglows" that follow each evening's entertainment, everyone is perpetually numbed and loose, but a clubbish decorum prevails just the same. No one throws up. Now and then, though, a Bohemian sits down in the ferns and passes out. The sense that you are inside an actual club is heightened by all the furnishings that could not survive a wet season outdoors: the stuffed lion on top of Jungle camp; the red lanterns in the trees behind Dragons camp at night, which add to the haunting atmosphere. ... Bohemians talk about roughing it, but at a privy in the woods near the river, there is a constantly renewed supply of paper toilet-seat covers.

WASHOE HOUSE

Sonoma lore holds that a westernmost Civil War episode took place at Washoe House, the venerable saloon still standing on Stony Point Road. A Unionist posse from Petaluma [they say] headed north to have done with pro-Confederate Santa Rosa. But with a stop for refreshment here [they say], their resolve vanished in the bottom of a glass, forestalling the planned attack. Sadly, there seems to be little documentation for the tale, though that does not prevent many retellings.

BOTTLES OF NOTE

BUENA VISTA 1857 California's debut vintage, likely combining many grape varieties imported by Count Haraszthy.

FAR NIENTE 1886 *Sweet Muscat* A bottle turned up in a Marin County cellar in 1998, an exceptionally ancient discovery.

INGLENOOK 1941 *Cabernet Sauvignon* Nabbing perfect scores and Christie's bids into the 2000s. Recent bottle price: $27,000.

SAN ANTONIO ALTAR WINE *Circa* 1925 Only 40 Napa wineries survived Prohibition. San Antonio got by on sacramental wine, remains a top producer.

ROBERT MONDAVI FUMÉ BLANC 1968 A genius rebrand of sauvignon blanc [once deemed boring] by modern Napa's inventor.

ITALIAN SWISS COLONY *Circa* 1955 Classic jug wine, rope-wrapped teardrop bottle. Ad slogan inspired Dean Martin croon: "The little ole wine drinker—me."

CHARLES SHAW 1987 *Gamay Beaujolais* "As beautiful as a vase of fresh-cut flowers." —*LA Times*. Brand predecessor to Two-Buck Chuck.

BEAULIEU VINEYARD 1968 *Georges De Latour Private Reserve* Revered cabernet sauvignon still inspires tasting-note rapture. Hunt around.

CHATEAU MONTELENA 1973 *Chardonnay* Patriotic education: Mike Grgich's chard beat the French at the landmark '76 Paris tasting.

KENDALL-JACKSON 1982 *Vintner's Reserve Chardonnay* Sonoma grapes joined the cross-Cali blend that made chards a Reagan-era staple.

ETUDE 1992 *Pinot Noir Dry Rosé* Winemaker Tony Soter opens the floodgates of today's "summer water" obsession.

SCREAMING EAGLE 1992 *Cabernet Sauvignon* Catalyst of '90s cult-wine boom of high prices, rare bottles. [Bonné: "a neutron bomb."] Six-liter sold at 2000 auction for $500,000.

ALMANAC

MORNING STAR RANCH

Time
July 7, 1967

An hour's drive north of San Francisco, in apple-growing country near Sebastopol along the Russian River, some 30 to 50 country hippies live on a 31-acre ranch called Morning Star. Their closest neighbor: Cartoonist Charles Schulz, whose *Peanuts* people are hippie favorites. The ranch is owned by Lou Gottlieb, 43, former arranger, composer and bassist for the folk-singing Limeliters, who has his hippie followers hard at work—rarest of all hippie trips—growing vegetables for the San Francisco Diggers. Most Morning Star colonists avoid acid. "I'd rather have beautiful children than beautiful visions," says a tanned, clear-eyed hippie girl named Joan. That hippies can actually work becomes evident on a tour of the commune's vegetable gardens. Cabbages and turnips, lettuce and onions march in glossy green rows, neatly mulched with redwood sawdust. Hippie girls lounge in the buffalo grass, sewing colorful dresses or studying Navajo sand painting, clad in nothing but beads, bells and feather headdresses. [Not everyone is a nudist—only when they feel like it.] A shaggy sheepdog named Grass plays with the hippie children, among them a straw-thatched 17-month-old boy named Adam Siddhartha.

FALCON CREST

Known for wild cliffhangers and pungent dialogue, the prime-time soap tracked the "Tuscany Valley" elite from 1981 to 1990. Select moments:

SEASON 1: A death triggers dynastic struggle between steely Falcon Crest winery matriarch Angela Channing [Jane Wyman] and upstart nephew Chase Gioberti [Robert Foxworth].

SEASON 2: Shots fired at a wedding reception. Fade to a coffin lowering into the earth. But … whose?

SEASON 7: False deaths. Mysterious figures. Abductions. Explosions. A stock market plot! Amid the chaos, can Angela keep control of Falcon Crest?

ANGELA CHANNING SPEAKS: "Revenge leaves a very bitter taste in one's mouth. Something like sour grapes. Why don't you leave it to the pros?"

TO-KALON VINEYARD

1868	H.W. Crabb plants Oakville-area vineyard; boasts largest U.S. grape variety collection
1884	Crabb's cabernet sauvignon: one of Napa's first significant cabs
1886	Name "To-Kalon" adopted, meaning, in Greek, "the place of highest beauty"
1903	USDA starts research vineyard on property, resulting in gold-medal wines
1943	SF businessman Martin Stelling plants new vines on part of original property
1944	Stelling acquires more of original parcel, plus extends property
1962	Mondavi wine clan buys some original Crabb land and Stelling Extension acreage
1977	After family feud settlement, Robert Mondavi holds Stelling-era chunk
1993	Andy Beckstoffer, vineyard baron, buys To-Kalon section
2002	Legal battle as Mondavi, Beckstoffer both lay claim to To-Kalon name
2020	Mondavi claims "To Kalon" is a brand. Beckstoffer, others say it's a place.

SOUTHERN POMO

Southern Pomo was spoken by thousands along the Russian River and the Pacific coast. Russia's Fort Ross colony brought long-term European contact; later, Spanish, Mexican and American settlers brought slavery and death. By 1900, most Southern Pomo people had been killed. Survivors passed on their culture, however, and today, Southern Pomo peoples are working to regain their language.

A small Southern Pomo sampler:

KAS:IN redwood tree
NO:MI cottontail rabbit
ŠAK:A:KA California quail

K'A:YAN duck
LE:LE forehead
MIS:IBO three

CESAR CHAVEZ

"ANOTHER GROWER FALLS"
El Malcriado [*English-language edition*], *April 21, 1966*

Another major grape grower signed an agreement with Cesar Chavez. The Christian Brothers, makers of Christian Brothers Wine, own a big winery and hundreds of acres of land in the Napa Valley. ... They announced their field workers would be protected by the N.F.W.A., and that a written contract would be signed within a few weeks. Brother Gregory, president of Mont La Salle Vineyards, the main vineyards covered by the agreement, said, "We are prepared to formally recognize the N.F.W.A. as the organization through which social justice may be realized for our agricultural workers." The Christian Brothers are a Catholic religious order, and there was no strike or threat of strike at their vineyards. But the field workers there need higher wages, just like everywhere else. There are over 200 workers during harvest season [and at one time braceros were used]. Like all farm workers, they need a union to protect them and their rights. Brother Gregory stressed that the union was recognized voluntarily, because the Christian Brothers knew that the workers' cause was just. ... The Christian Brothers tried to get the other growers in the Napa Valley to voluntarily sign a contract, the other growers refused.

> *In 2015, statues of Chavez and United Farm Workers co-founder Dolores Huerta, created by Napa sculptor Mario Chiodo, were unveiled in Veterans Memorial Park. Union representation remains an industry issue, along with immigration enforcement, mechanization and health concerns.*

JOHN GRIDER

Born enslaved in Tennessee in 1826, John Grider lived a long arc of California history. In great old age he told the Black historian Delilah Bailey that it was he who found the paint for the Bear Flag; of the Sonoma revolt itself, he recalled, "It did not amount to much." In 1914, he was lauded by the Native Sons of the Golden West. On his death in '24, the near-centenarian was noted as one of the last eyewitnesses to modern California's birth.

HANNAH WEINBERGER

After a disgruntled employee murdered her husband in 1882, Hannah Weinberger became Napa's first woman winemaker. Just seven years later, she won a silver medal at the world's fair in Paris—the only California vintner honored at the event. Prohibition closed the Weinberger operation. Now, the 35 acres Weinberger oversaw belong to William Cole Vineyards in St. Helena.

THE SEA RANCH

Progressive Architecture, March 1967

Graphic designer Barbara Stauffacher … arrived at the Sea Ranch resort development, Sonoma County, California, with pots of purple, red, black, and blue paint, two sign painters, and a tentative scheme. Her assignment was to dress up the resort community's bathhouse.… "Much of the design," says Mrs. Stauffacher, "was done on the spot, since there are so many angles and views that could not be calculated beforehand. I … drew a lot of lines on the walls with charcoal and string, and they painted in the colors I wanted. Whenever I'd ask Mattie Silva [Sea Ranch's builder] if it was getting to be too much, he'd say, 'No, kid, make it happy.'" The graphics grew out of the architectural forms and out of Mrs. Stauffacher's own vocabulary of signs: Arrows lead into each side of the building, up the stairs; stripes progress around corners. The motifs make the rooms appear bigger and visually reinforce the beams, roof angles, and multiple levels that were lost when the rooms were all white.… "It's a bit like a three-dimensional internal sculpture house that you can walk into," explains Mrs. Stauffacher, "and it's a bit of a shocker: The exterior is all wood and shingles. The inside is a kinesthetic world of shapes and colors."

> *The Sea Ranch is a notable preserve of midcentury design thinking, its low-slung, wood-clad buildings harmonizing with the Sonoma Coast landscape. "Supergraphics" by Barbara Stauffacher [now Solomon] are one of the community's signatures. Search out the University of California's extraordinary digital archive* Journey to the Sea Ranch.

ALMANAC

THE FRENCH LAUNDRY

Thomas Keller's Yountville restaurant is revered for triple-Michelin excellence, famed for steep prices and elusive reservations.

TASTING MENU SELECTIONS
[*From September 23, 2020*]

Garden Cauliflower "Velouté"
[*Sweet Onions and Preserved Périgord Black Winter Truffles*]

Sweet Butter Poached Alaskan King Crab
[*Marinated Garden Tomatoes, Crispy Chickpea "Panisse," Fragrant Basil and Spicy Tomato Broth*]

"Mac and Cheese"
[*Hand Cut Macaroni, Parmesan "Mousseline" and Preserved Périgord Black Winter Truffles*] $125.00 *supplement*

RAVE

"[A]n old stone house filled with the golden light of many candles… and on fine nights tables are set in the fragrant garden beneath a starry sky.… Every chef in the world fantasizes about a place just like that. But Thomas Keller did more. Three years ago, he bought a restaurant called the French Laundry in the Napa Valley and made the dream come true."

—*Ruth Reichl,* The New York Times, *October 29, 1997*

CRITIQUE

"RESERVATIONS NIGHTMARE! I have been trying to get through to The French Laundry Reservations Line from the UK for the past 4 hours! I booked the trip 9 months ago as a surprise for my husband's 40th Birthday. I called the reservation line on the exact date [2 calendar months before] and was greeted by an answerphone message to advise that they were closed until July 20th. I have even called the international operator to see if they could help but alas no!… I am absolutely gutted."

—*One-star review, TripAdvisor, July 19, 2005*

THE MONDAVIS

The most iconic, successful and dysfunctional family in American winemaking features all the elements of delicious drama and a rags-to-riches dream arc. An immigrant strikes gold with a brilliant investment. [Cesare, the first patriarch, packed grapes for home vintners as C. Mondavi & Sons, then bought Napa bastion Charles Krug.] A notorious fist-fight over the future. [Sons Robert and Peter brawled in 1965, and Robert split away to found Napa's first truly modern winery.] A viticultural visionary and brilliant booster whose financial freewheeling ripped the family fabric. A contentious public trial, a massive sellout and, of course, millions of dollars at stake, always. The family saga tracks Napa Valley's development into a world-class wine region, from waves of Italian immigration through Prohibition, into the late-20th-century boom. Even now, winemakers large to small will still invoke Robert's name with reverence. Meanwhile, the Mondavi brand long since became an empire, riding market forces to global prominence while arguably diluting its reputation. After a billion-dollar sale to a conglomerate in 2004, a younger generation pursues viticultural passions under several new labels [Raen, Continuum], among other ventures [fine art, driverless tractors].

ANTI-CHINESE BIGOTRY

"THE COOLIE QUESTION. — Napa valley, as everyone knows, will one day be as great a producer of California wine and wine brandy as any county of its size in the state ... If Chinamen are introduced ... many a family will have the bread of life dashed from their lips by the jeweled hand of the Mongolian capitalist." —*Daily Evening Reporter,* April 29, 1867

"The tallow-colored rat-eaters of the celestial empire, we noticed while in Napa, are investing largely in revolvers. They evince a determination to fight their way to the Flowery Kingdom." —*St. Helena Star,* December 10, 1874

> *Chinese workers provided vital labor to the early California wine industry but were targeted by exclusionary policy as well as racist abuse. The state's 1913 Alien Land Law prevented immigrants from China, Japan and elsewhere from owning agricultural land.*

PROHIBITION

The days of a century back, more or less, were not such glamorous times for California wine country. After weathering the pendulum swings of price-plummeting oversupply and the scourge of phylloxera, which decimated the California immigrant communities' Old World vines, winemakers faced Prohibition. On January 16, 1920, the *Napa Daily Journal* opined: "King Barleycorn is supposedly dead all over the United States after today." [The paper also took note of a great push to stock up.] Of the 700-plus operations in wine country before Prohibition, only about 40 made it. Survivors wiggled through loopholes in the Volstead Act. They could supply the Communion needs of the Catholic Church, or they could sell the juice of grapes for, presumably, other bootlegging winemakers to ferment under the table. [In '23, Georges de Latour, of the historically vital house Beaulieu, was able to plant new vines, so healthy was the trade in "sacramental" wines.] Once the 18th Amendment was repealed, in 1933, it wasn't exactly boom times, as the Great Depression weighed heavy on national conviviality. But reborn from legal doom—and, some say, boosted by World War II's freeze on European imports—the region's wine industry slowly began to take the shape we know today.

ROBERT LOUIS STEVENSON

Wine in California is still in the experimental stage; and when you taste a vintage, grave economical questions are involved. The beginning of vine-planting is like the beginning of mining for the precious metals: the wine-grower also "prospects." One corner of land after another is tried with one kind of grape after another. This is a failure; that is better; a third best. … The smack of Californian earth shall linger on the palate of your grandson. Meanwhile the wine is merely a good wine; the best that I have tasted better than a Beaujolais, and not unlike. But the trade is poor; it lives from hand to mouth, putting its all into experiments, and forced to sell its vintages. … All things in this new land are moving further on: the wine-vats and the miner's blasting tools but picket for a night, like Bedouin pavilions; and to-morrow, to fresh woods! This stir of change and these perpetual echoes of the moving footfall, haunt the land. Men move eternally, still chasing Fortune; and, Fortune found, still wander. —*The Silverado Squatters* [1883]

THE RUSSIANS

A Journal of a Round the World Voyage on the Sloop Kamchatka
by Fyodor F. Matiushkin

On September 21, 1818, we sighted Bodega Bay. Four Aleuts who were with us were given presents, and we sent them ashore; in the face of a strong south-southeast wind we reached the entrance and dropped anchor. There is an outpost there, in a rather small cove, which has been named after Count Rumiantsev. A brig with the same name is also there, built by simple *promyshleniks* who have no experiences in shipbuilding. Its navigator … welcomed us with a seven-gun salute and soon came out to meet us himself. He was quite pleased to see some compatriots and many acquaintances in isolation. He and two Russian *promyshleniks* live alone here on board ship. There are no buildings at Rumiantsev Bay, except for a single warehouse. Even the natives, who live a roving life, often leave them behind, and they become quite like orphans in this desolate and distant corner of the earth.

I saw a puff of smoke from behind a small promontory. I climbed it and saw a band of New Albion nomads. They all looked at me, but since I was aware of their peace-loving nature and special affection toward Russians, I approached them boldly. These people get everything from nature without the slightest effort. Born in a temperate, fair climate, they need no clothing. Most remarkable of all are their boats, which are made of rushes. When someone sits on them [not in them, for they are tied together like little floats and you sit on top of them] and sets a net, the whole boat submerges, and sometimes no more than a head is visible above the water. … The strength and speed with which they shoot their arrows is extraordinary; once let fly, they instantly disappear from view.

After I walked along the shore a bit more, it began to get dark, and I headed back. The entire expanse around Bodega Bay is completely desolate. On the most distant ridges evergreen stands are visible, but here only low shrubs grow, along with a great profusion of pretty flowers, which give off a pleasant fragrance toward evening.

> *Between 1812 and 1841, the Russian Empire colonized Sonoma's Fort Ross, indenturing Aleutian and Californian Indigenous people to hunt sea otters. [Otter populations were devastated.] For more, consult the Fort Ross Conservancy's digital archives.*

INGLENOOK

1879.... Finnish sea captain Gustave Niebaum founds Inglenook, staked by Alaska fur exploits. In Rutherford, he builds château winery, imports fine vines, French techniques.

1892.... The '92 vintage: "floral, dried-cherry quality." [Tasted in 2001, *Wine Spectator*.]

1908.... Gustave dies, widow Suzanne takes charge. *Napa* author Conaway's description: "a steel rod in black bombazine."

1914.... John Daniel Jr. becomes aunt Suzanne's ward after his mother dies.

1915.... At canal celebration Panama-Pacific International Exposition, Inglenook romps: 19 gold medals.

1933.... Inglenook hosts all-day Repeal celebration; '33 cabernet soon on market. Vine preservation during Prohibition deemed "miracle."

1939.... Daniel now supervises, achieving prestige $2/bottle price tag. War embargos soon push cabernet to $3.50. Watchwords: "Pride, not profit."

1950s .. Mounting financial, infrastructural woes.

1964.... Daniel sells Inglenook to massive United Vintners, shocking Napa. Price: $1.2 million.

1969.... Heublein, maker of Smirnoff Vodka, buys brand. Varieties blended down to legal minimum [51 percent].

1970.... Daniel dies. Widow sells estate land for planned golf course [never built].

1975.... Filmmaker Francis Ford Coppola invests *Godfather* loot in portion of original Inglenook property.

1980s .. Corporate horse trades turn Inglenook into a cheap jug-wine brand.

1995.... Coppola, aided by *Bram Stoker's Dracula* proceeds, buys château, reunifying estate.

2011.... Coppola acquires Inglenook brand name, heralding efforts to replant clones of original Niebaum vines.

2020.... Robin Daniel Lail, daughter of John, is founder and owner of Lail Vineyards, continuing dynasty.

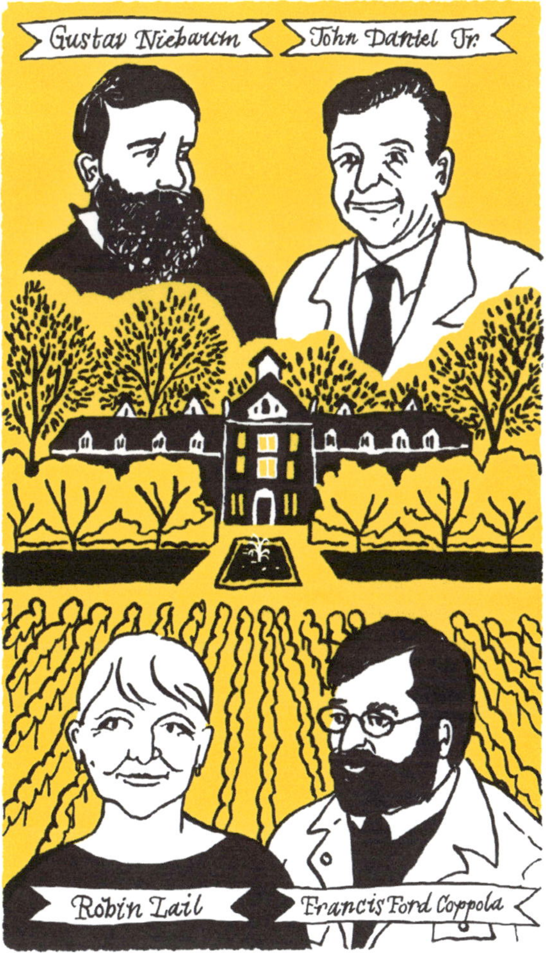
Gustav Niebaum
John Daniel Jr.
Robin Lail
Francis Ford Coppola

"GENTLEMEN VINTNERS OF CALIFORNIA"

By Frank Cameron [from manuscript, circa 1961]

In California's warm world of the vine and the grape, and most of the country's best-known wineries, there is a tiny cluster of private wine-makers who, with their hearts and their skills, are producing custom wines as good as or better than some of Europe's best. ... Perhaps the most colorful of these estate vineyards is that of Frank H. Bartholomew, chairman of the board of United Press International, and his wife, Toni. Set in the Valley of the Moon, north of San Francisco, the Barthlomews' Buena Vista winery is drenched in sun, history, atmosphere, and romance. ... To American wine-lovers, the sainted name that attaches itself to the Barthlomews' Buena Vista is that of the Hungarian count, Agoston Haraszthy. He not only built its wineries and stocked some of its fields, but is revered as the father of modern California viticulture ... At Buena Vista, along with a few of Haraszthy's original roots, are his two stone wineries built in a hillside beneath oaks and eucalyptus. In their cool, dim depths, picked out by Chinese labor so long ago, the wines placidly mature in huge, ancient casks of Limousin oak and Circassian walnut that know neither nail nor rivet. On the face of one appears the winemaker's universal philosophy:

Back of the wine is the vintner,
And back through the years his skill,
And back of it all are the vines in the sun
And the rain and the Master's will.

CALIFORNIA VS. EUROPE

While 1976's "Judgement of Paris" tasting is famed, comparison is an old game. James Zellerbach received this letter while serving as U.S. ambassador to Rome.

"Dear Mr. Ambassador — I want to tell you of an experiment I made on Saturday night with the wine you gave me. I had five guests for dinner and before they sat down at the table I poured your wine properly chilled into one glass for each of them and in another glass ... Corton Charlemagne 1955. I asked them to tell me which was which. These people are quite knowledgeable on French wines and generally have a dim view of California wine. Three out of the five picked your wine as the Burgundy and the Burgundy as the California wine." —*Morrill Cody, September. 26, 1960*

THE BIRDS

Released in 1963 to mostly positive reviews, Alfred Hitchcock's ominous tale of feathered friends turned foes takes place in Sonoma County's Bodega Bay.

THE NEW YORK TIMES

"Tippi Hedren is pretty, bland and wholesome as the disruptive girl. Rod Taylor is stolid and sturdy as the mother-smothered son. Jessica Tandy is querulous as the mother, and pretty Suzanne Pleshette is pleasant but vaguely sinister as the old girl friend. There are the usual Hitchcock 'characters' spotted through the film. And those birds! Well, you've never seen such actors! They are amazingly malevolent feathered friends." —*Bosley Crowther*

THE HOLLYWOOD REPORTER

"The revolt of the birds, acting contrary to nature and their established habits, is convincingly presented. The fact that birds are the last element of nature one expects to turn on man only underlines the horror. If you can't trust birds, who can you trust?" —*James Powers*

TIME

"[T]he most unforgettable performers in *The Birds* are the birds. They are utterly, terrifyingly believable as they go about their bloody business of murdering humanity. Pigeons loitering around the exits of theaters where this movie is shown would be wise to lie low until the next change of feature." —*Staff*

> *For a nitty-gritty documentary look at the contemporary wine trade and vineyard culture in Napa Valley, see the 2016 film* Decanted, *by director Nick Kovacic.*

ALMANAC

ROBERT PARKER

Today's Napa, global destination, didn't come out of thin air. In fact, many identify one man—sometimes, through gritted purple teeth—as the catalyst. Robert Parker, a Marylander with scant traditional qualifications, made himself the world's most influential wine critic. As founder of *The Wine Advocate*, Parker installed a 100-point rating system that remains iconic. In the 1990s and 2000s, his influence waxed, such that even as France awarded him a Legion of Honor medal, the entire region of Burgundy blacklisted him for alleged offense to one cellar. Parker posits himself as an outsider of no formal training, a masterless warrior against mass industrialization, an advocate for less-filtered, small-production vintages. However, his dream to "democratize" wine by treating $20 and $200 bottles to the same blind scrutiny actually made a monarchy of sorts, as winemakers swayed their styles to gain Parker's approving nod. One high score could quadruple sales. How did this influence Napa? Parker is often blamed for steering the valley toward dense, dark, jammy, oaky, high-alcohol wines, a style as synonymous with the '90s as a Kenny G riff. But Parker was just one voice, with the land's terroir and American tastes for the bodacious also in play. A titan until retirement in 2019, Parker's long shadow still casts much of winemaking in its shade.

UC DAVIS

Chat up enough winemakers and observers of the California scene and perspectives on the University of California, Davis inevitably arise. The school, founded in 1905 to teach the agricultural sciences, runs the nation's best-known viticulture program, a magnet for vintners with Big Wine ambitions. In its modern incarnation, Davis has been credited for bringing Napa Valley wine country back from the brink of Prohibition extinction and for influencing some of California's biggest winemakers. Yet Davis receives looks askance, too. Some believe the school's scientific approaches push wine toward homogeneity—toward a bland industrialism. In recent years, however, winemakers noted for their dedication to "natural" techniques have passed through the rigorous program. [Sebastopol's Martha Stoumen, for example.] With deep archives, a sprawling network of connections and a mission to advance the winemaking art, Davis wields influence as varied and nuanced as it is inescapable.

AGOSTON HARASZTHY

Shortly after founding Sonoma's Buena Vista winery in 1857, "Count" Haraszthy surveyed European wines to assess California's potential.

Various examinations confirmed my previous conviction, that California is superior in all the conditions of soil, climate, and other natural advantages, to the most favored wine-producing districts of Europe, and that it actually has yielded considerably more per acre. All this State requires to produce a generous and noble wine is the varieties of grapes from which the most celebrated wines are made, and the same care and science in its manufacture. ... California can produce as noble and generous a wine as any in Europe; more quantity to the acre, and without repeated failures through frosts, summer rains, hailstorms, or other causes. —*Grape Culture, Wines, and Wine-Making* [1862]

JACK LONDON

Wander with me through one mood of the myriad of moods of sadness into which one is plunged by John Barleycorn. I ride out over my beautiful ranch. Between my legs is a beautiful horse. The air is wine. The grapes on a score of rolling hills are red with autumn flame. Across Sonoma Mountain wisps of sea fog are stealing. The afternoon sun smoulders in the drowsy sky. I have everything to make me glad I am alive. I am filled with dreams and mysteries. I am all sun and air and sparkle. I am vitalized, organic. I move, I have the power of movement, I command movement of the live thing I bestride. ... And yet, with a jaundiced eye I gaze upon all the beauty and wonder about me, and with jaundiced brain consider the pitiful figure I cut in this world that endured so long without me and will again endure without me. I remember the men who broke their hearts and their backs over this stubborn soil that now belongs to me. ... These men passed. I, too, shall pass. — *John Barleycorn* [1913]

> *London [1876–1916] schooled himself into a chronicler of working California. [Stints as oyster pirate and sealer deckhand salt his résumé.] He bestowed the poetic name "the Valley of the Moon" upon Sonoma, where he spent his waning years on Beauty Ranch, now* **JACK LONDON STATE HISTORIC PARK**. *John Barleycorn is considered autobiographical.*

INCLUDED

- 062 *California wine foundations*
- 063 *Timeline*
- 064 *Soils and Geography*
- 065 *Wine production*
- 066 *Tasting how-to*
- 067 *Napa and Sonoma winery picks*
- 070 *Winemaker Perspectives*

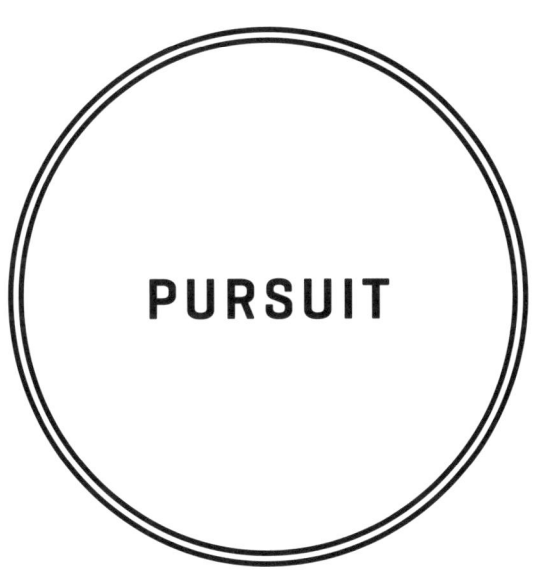

PURSUIT

A field guide to wine in Napa and Sonoma, with historical background, technical insight and a curated selection of fine makers in both counties

WINE HISTORY

In Northern California wine, ancient earth-building intersects with the latest marketing trends. Behind bold-face reputations and a glossy surface lies a true farming culture stitched from hard work, generational knowledge and expert craft.

FOUNDATIONS

CULTURE

Russian colonists planted grapes at Sonoma's Fort Ross in 1817, and Spanish missionaries sewed vineyards throughout the state in the 1820s. Immigration, particularly of Italians and, notably, Italian-speaking Swiss, embedded winemaking in the region's culture. Meanwhile, Chinese [historically] and Latinx workers [now] provide vital labor; Hispanic-owned wineries are on the rise. After trials—the vine-killing phylloxera bug and Prohibition—wine revived as mass-market product and high-craft art for '70s cachet and a long boom born of the '90s.

CLIMATE

Awash in sun, these valleys near the sea have a daily special guest: rolling fog layers, which cool vines overnight and protect them from morning heat. Ocean winds rush inland through the Petaluma Gap. The coastal influence also gives Sonoma and Napa a large "diurnal shift": day-to-night swings up to 40 degrees, lengthening the growing season. The climate varies here from coastal cool to Mediterranean heat, creating many microclimates, each influencing what goes in the bottle—a constant wine-trade talking point.

GEOLOGY

Cataclysmic events shaped this landscape, from the subduction of the Farallon plate to eruptions and earthquakes caused by the San Andreas Fault. Volcanic ash formed valleys and ridges. Inland seas receded into the Pacific over millennia, leaving alluvial fans to settle and resettle. The region contains half of the world's known soil orders, and ghostly remnants of ancient waters are found throughout the valleys. Variety supports a great diversity of grapes.

TIMELINE

Primordial... Ancient seas, rivers, eruptions deposit future *terroir*
A.D. 500 .... Patwin, Miwok, other Indigenous peoples thrive in region
1769 .... Missionaries plant California's first wine grapes [Mission]
1776 .... Spanish fort near present-day Napa
1817 .... Russian-American Company plants vines at Fort Ross
1836 .... Trapper George Yount: first U.S. settler in Napa Valley
1846 .... Bear Flag Revolt and U.S. seizure of present-day California
1848 .... Gold rush expands wine market [among other effects]
1857 .... Haraszthy builds cellars, launches Sonoma's Buena Vista
1861 .... Charles Krug founds winery in St. Helena, Napa County
1862 .... German Jacob Schram plants grapes near Calistoga
1863 .... Phylloxera louse exported to Europe, vines devastated
1872 .... Phylloxera infests Napa Valley grape vines
1882 .... Hannah Weinberger: first female Napa winemaker
1900 .... De Latours found Beaulieu, import louse-resistant rootstock
1920 .... Prohibition. Demand for fresh grapes mysteriously rises
1933 .... Repeal. UC Davis soon relaunches viticulture program
1938 .... André Tchelistcheff joins Beaulieu. Mentor to many
1943 .... Petri Wine sponsors *Sherlock Holmes*, Rathbone radio vehicle
1960 .... Dry wine outsells sweet wine in U.S., a modern first
1960s .... Italian Swiss Colony's "Little Old Winemaker": TV ad icon
1965 .... Jamie and Jack Davis revive long-dormant Schramsberg
1966 .... Robert Mondavi founds Napa's first post-Prohibition winery
1968 .... Napa Agricultural Preserve protects vineyards
1976 .... "Judgement of Paris" tasting: Napa wines beat the French
1978 .... Orson Welles' Paul Masson TV ads. Worth a search
1981 .... Phylloxera afflicts the AxR#1 rootstock, sparking alarm
.... First Napa Valley Wine Auction nets $141,000
1990 .... Harlan Estate: cult-wine trendsetter, $1,000 bottle maker
2004 .... According to legend, *Sideways* crushes merlot, boosts pinot
2015 .... Napa Wine Auction bags record $6M; John Legend performs
2020 .... Glass Fire ravages Napa, Sonoma. Historic wineries destroyed

SOILS OF NOTE

Soil is key to terroir, a concept that blends science and mystique to link wine flavor to where vines take root. A regional dirt typology:

Marine Soils	Northern California is partly old ocean floor. Receding inland seas left fossils, a complex mosaic of soils to fuel diverse winemakers' ambitions.
Rutherford Bench	A gravelly ancient streambed. Since the 1936 Beaulieu Vineyard Reserve, home to world-beating cabernets.
Volcanic Soils	The San Andreas Fault caused major eruptions starting 9 million years ago, leaving basalt and volcanic debris, high in mineral nutrients.
Steinbeck Series	Loam formed from alluvial sandstone runoff, mainly in Petaluma. Supports long growing seasons. Name: a bonus.
Huichica Series	Fine loam with clay subsoil, formed of volcanic ash and sedimentary alluvium. Well-drained topsoil, but retains water for hotter vineyards.
Goldridge Series	Famous in Green Valley, fine sandy loam with coarse sandstone underneath, perfect planting in wetter coastal zones.
Carneros Clay	Among California's youngest soils, fertile with sediment from one of the last inland seas to recede into the Pacific.

GEOGRAPHY

Geographer Patrick Shabram explains:
"AMERICAN VITICULTURAL AREAS *meet two basic criteria: They're known grape-growing regions, and they're geographically distinct. How different is the climate on one side of a highway from the other? Often, not much. Yet the overall characteristics on one side are different, so you use the highway as your boundary.*"

PRODUCTION CYCLE

Wine's creation combines agriculture, science and blue-collar hard work.

HARVEST Late summer commences a frenzy of activity. Grapes are often harvested at night, in cooler temps, to retain their acidity. Unlike avocados or bananas, grapes do not ripen off the vine. Timing is crucial. **KEY JOB:** *seasonal field worker*

SORTING Grapes go to a vibrating table, a tool for eliminating rotten or unripe grapes, leaves and debris, all known as MOG [material other than grapes]. **KEY JOB:** *harvest intern*

FERMENTATION, PART 1 Yeasts digest natural sugars and excrete alcohol. Crushed red-wine grapes ferment with their skins to extract color and tannin, abiding in aromatic vats. Carbon dioxide pushes skins to the surface, creating a "cap" that must be punched down [pigeage] or pumped over [remontage] to keep extraction going. **KEY JOB:** *enologist*

FERMENTATION, PART 2 In malolactic fermentation [MLF], bacteria [not yeast] digest malic acid [think tart green apple taste] and create lactic acid [think cream] to yield "rounder," smoother red-wine flavors. Rare for whites, but very popular for Napa chardonnay, creating noted buttery qualities. **KEY JOB:** *winemaker*

PRESS Wine that drains off the grapes—"free run" juice—is best quality. Grapes are pressed to extract the remnant juice, often blended with free run or bottled as a different wine. **KEY TOOL:** *pomace shovel*

ÉLEVAGE Aging time varies per grape variety, desired wine style and winemaker aesthetic. Wine ages in barrels, tanks [stainless steel or cement] or ceramic amphorae. Testing, additions and blending occur to achieve desired flavor. **KEY TOOL:** *wine thief*

BOTTLING Wine may be filtered before bottling. Many wines go through some aging in the bottle before they go on the market. **KEY JOB:** *forklift operator*

TASTING

Key points of interest, how-to steps and vocabulary for winetasting.

WHITE WINE

APPEARANCE Hold wine at an angle over blank paper to consider color. *Descriptors: gold, green, silver, lemon, orange*

AROMA Primary aromas come from grapes: fruit and earth. Common: *Golden Delicious apples, lemon zest, white mushrooms*. Secondary aromas [*butter, vanilla*] come from winemaking, including MLF and oak use. Tertiary [e.g., *dried apricot* or *caramel*]: from bottle aging and oxidation.

PALATE Consider texture. Is wine *light*, or does it coat your mouth [*creamy*]? Gauge other primary fruit flavors, secondary and tertiary flavors from aging. To consider *acidity*, hold liquid against the roof of your mouth; see if your mouth waters. In a Napa chardonnay, find *lemon zest, butter* flavors from MLF, *vanilla* from oak aging.

ORIGIN Is wine "vineyard-designate"—all grapes from one vineyard? Is it a "Napa County" wine, or from a specific AVA [e.g., Stags Leap, Mount Veeder]? Did grapes grow on a slope, or the valley floor? Sun exposure will affect how ripe—therefore, how *full*—the wine is.

RED WINE

APPEARANCE Swirl wine to see if it "paints" glass, how slowly it moves [viscosity]. *Descriptors: red, purple, garnet, ruby, tawny*

AROMA Primary notes can include *strawberries, cassis, blueberries, forest floor*. Secondary aromas show up as *cloves, vanilla, bramble, cedar, stewed fruits*. Examples of tertiary aromas in red wines that have been bottle-aged: *leather, tobacco, prunes*.

PALATE Hold a sip on your tongue, relate sensation to nonfat or whole milk. *Full-bodied* wine will evoke whole milk, heavy on the tongue. Tannins are perceived in the back of your mouth. May induce clenched jaw. Think fruit, earth and spices. In a Napa cabernet, you might taste *black currant, licorice* or *cinnamon* from oak.

WINEMAKING Was the wine de-stemmed, or did it undergo carbonic maceration, fermenting uncrushed? How long was fermentation? For rosés, how long was skin contact? Was wine aged in oak, stainless steel, cement, amphorae? Filtered? Such techniques affect final flavor.

BESTS: WINE

*There can be no last work on Napa and Sonoma wine.
To get the first word, we asked around [and pulled corks] for names
to know, places to go and bottles to seek.*

CLASSIC NAPA Joseph Phelps
Former cattle ranch, now the epitome of family-run Napa.

....

NEW NAPA The Terraces
Fresh ideas on a historic spread, including a "ghost winery."

....

CLASSIC SONOMA Gundlach Bundschu
Meticulous sustainable farming going back to 1858.

....

NEW SONOMA Jolie-Laide
Rare varieties [valdiguié] shred in ex–Chicago skateboarder's hands.

....

WILD CARD Drinkward Peschon
Specialized collaboration by two renowned winemakers: one killer cab.

PURSUIT

NAPA

CLASSIC

CORISON
Cathy Corison, revered figure, wields Napa cab power without bombast.

SPOTTSWOODE
Come here for that old glow: vintage architecture, family stories, winning cabernet.

SKY VINEYARDS
Literally off-grid, way up Mount Veeder for six decades. Zins and syrahs.

CHATEAU MONTELENA
Core spot: founded by a gold rush rope tycoon, Judgement of Paris winner.

HEITZ CELLAR
A '60s-vintage stalwart with sharp young leaders. Bright, velvety chardonnay.

BROWN ESTATE
Black-owned trailblazer, family-founded in 1980. Noted for zinfandel.

FROG'S LEAP
Philosophical, painstaking care for soil and flavor [i.e., terroir]. Classic '70s/'80s backstory.

NEW

MATTHIASSON
Much-lauded. One of the radical voices redefining Napa style.

ODETTE
Lavish, well-regarded Stags Leap District spread. Co-owned by the governor.

DIRTY AND ROWDY
Southern transplants with bodacious attitude and a way with the tricky mourvedre.

ASHES & DIAMONDS
An airy embassy of enlightened design and spot-on winemaking.

MASSICAN
Top winemaker Dan Petroski's sunny, Italian-style white wine.

TURLEY
Winemaker Tegan Passalacqua: new-school approach to very old vines.

REALM
A boutique but formidable presence in the Stags Leap District. Arty, cult appeal.

SONOMA

CLASSIC

RIDGE
Midcentury icon, wines as exacting as the modernist labels. Geyserville zin blend is a good starting point.

HIRSCH
Long-standing cult go-to, farming remote and foggy coastal lands.

SEGHESIO
A California tale: Italian family, making wine since 1895. Venerable zins.

DEHLINGER
A small producer, one of Sonoma's key '70s industry revivalists. Estate pinot.

BUENA VISTA
Agoston Haraszthy's place, founded in 1857. A pilgrimage.

DONELAN
A hands-on family firm, result of a classic mid-career wine revelation.

CEJA
Center of a generational saga fit for the great Pan-American novel. Gushy, fun pinot.

NEW

MARTHA STOUMEN
Standard-bearer for cutting-edge natural wine and scholar of vines.

COBB
Pinot noir amid the Sonoma Coast redwoods. Winemaker Ross Cobb is a force.

SCRIBE
Need a mood boost? Report to this lush, whip-smart musing on place. Rosé of pinot, please.

REEVE
A wife, a husband, brainy pinot and chard. Check out Remy Saves the Sea, a white blend.

PEAY
Winemaker Vanessa Wong unravels Sonoma Coast pinot's many mysteries.

ENFIELD
John Lockwood hunts grapes across California; his Sonoma Coast cabs are notable.

APERTURE
Winemaker Jesse Katz is noted for a young-blood approach to Old World wine styles.

WINEMAKER PERSPECTIVES

"Because of its success, Napa not only *attracts* smart people, but in order to make it there, you have to *be* really smart. It's also a super-conventional place. One of the most conservative places I've ever been in my life. I don't mean politically. I mean culturally. I could not resist the opportunity to break away from that—and stay within it at the same time."

—ABE SCHOENER, Scholium Project [*ex–philosophy professor, known for experimental vintages*]

"There aren't that many industry towns—like LA with the film industry. Napa's such a small area, with so many winemakers and wineries packed together. People are so generous with their knowledge. They enjoy talking about it. If you were doing accounting, other accountants wouldn't want to talk about it over dinner. But talking about your vineyard, sharing each other's wine—that's different."

—SAMANTHA SHEEHAN, Poe Wines [*founder, inspired by French travels, winery name owes to ravens and the poet*]

"My father left his village at the age of 16. He became a U.S. citizen, started his own vineyard management company and became one of the top growers in Sonoma County. The most important thing he instilled in us was the importance of hard work, and to always be sincere. Sonoma County is special because of its diversity. We have so many different microclimates. The coast, redwoods, valleys—everything within driving distance."

—ELIZABETH VALDEZ, Valdez Family Winery [*took over winemaking after her father, Ulises, died, in* 2018]

"I absolutely love Sonoma County. I love the climate, the topography and that we get the best grapes. We have a relaxed ambience, reasonable prices for tastings and wines, and many small wineries, where the experience is much more intimate and pleasant. I love the crush process. I love getting my hands on the grapes. The hardest part initially was sales, but wine sells itself."

—OLGA FERNANDEZ, Guerrero Fernandez Winery [*emigrated from Morelia, tasting room in Windsor's Artisan Alley*]

INCLUDED

074 *Kashy Khaledi*
076 *Steve Sando*
077 *Elisa Hellenthal*
079 *Leslie Wiser*
080 *Kyle Connaughton*
081 *Shannon Shaffer-Killey*
082 *Tony Coturri*
085 *Arleene Correa Valencia*
086 *Andrew Mariani*
088 *Alexandria Brown*

INTERVIEWS

Ten conversations with locals of note about winemaking, lightning strikes, heritage vegetables, bean importation, migration, art, history and more

KASHY KHALEDI

WINERY FOUNDER

MY FIRST JOB was at Grand Royal Records, the Beastie Boys' label. I was 18. If you ordered an *Ill Communication* 12-inch vinyl in 1995 or '96, I put it in the envelope.

PEOPLE DON'T REALIZE how much warmth and inclusivity there was in punk. I was embraced by that community.

YOU DON'T SEE a bunch of punks at Ashes & Diamonds. But there's no velvet rope.

THE WINERY IS a reaction to what Napa Valley became. It's also a love letter to what it was.

IN THE MID-'60S, Robert Mondavi created hospitality in Napa Valley. We stand on his shoulders. We also appreciate the style of wine he made.

PEOPLE STARTED OVERLY manipulating their wines, going for higher alcohol. It's no longer a fresh product.

FRESHNESS comes from acidity. From earth tones.

BARBARA BESTOR, the architect, realized the vision: midcentury architecture inspired by the Case Study homes in California.

I THINK WE may have the lowest ceiling of any winery in Napa.

I WAS AT Capitol Records, in charge of artwork for albums, CDs, music videos, TV spots, what have you.

THERE'S A POLISH movie from the '50s, *Ashes and Diamonds*. The characters and visuals are incredible.

AN ASSASSIN HAS to choose between love and remaining an assassin. He doesn't choose love. I saw that as a cautionary tale.

LUSH GRASSES. Being enveloped in white and bright colors. The weightlessness you get from the zigzag structure above our tasting room.

IF YOU TRY one of our Mountain Cuvées, I call it "weightless power."

INTERVIEWS

STEVE SANDO

BEAN FARMER, IMPORTER

I WAS READY to get out of San Francisco, around 1999. Napa seemed like a nice small town.

IN RANCHO GORDO'S early days, someone at the farmers market said, "Oh, you should call it the Old Napa Bean Company, something like that." I'm like, "No, I'm not tying myself to Napa in any sense."

I HAD HAD all these jobs where I almost made it. I thought, screw it, I'm just going to make myself happy. I was going to get a job at Target and just have a garden. And that's when everything happened.

OUR SALES GROW about 20 percent every year. This year, way more. The Bean Club has 8,500 members, and the waiting list is 14,000.

VEGETABLES SHOULD be local. Dairy and meat should be regional. Grains and beans should grow where they grow best, because you don't have to rush them.

THE BEANS ARE ambassadors for Indigenous populations in Mexico that people wouldn't even know about.

MY PARTNERS IN Mexico initially thought I would tell them what beans we wanted. No, I want your grandmother's beans. I want them to be culturally relevant.

MY ATTITUDE IS, let's create opportunities. We're buying at market value. We're not overpaying, because our partners aren't a charity. But we keep coming back, year after year. We're all making money. That's the beautiful thing.

WHEN I COOK, I incorporate Asian, Mexican and European things. That is much more interesting to me.

THERE'S A DANGER, in Napa and Sonoma, of pretending we're only European. It all kind of wants to be Italy. But in fact, this was Mexico for a really long time.

ELISA HELLENTHAL

VINEYARD MANAGER

MY DAD, a logger by trade, saw there was open space on the property. A friend said, "Plant pinot noir."

DAD HAD NEVER worked with grapes or anything, but he thought, Why not?

AFTER HIGH SCHOOL, I wanted to go as far away as possible. I went to Seattle, studied photography. I remember the day I drove out to visit Mom and Dad. Beautiful day. Springtime. Everything was green.

WHY AM I not doing this?

DUST MITES ARE the worst thing we deal with. Powdery mildew is an issue, with the fog.

PRUNING IS THE most important thing. You're going not only for this year, but for next year, too. I prune the cordon myself. It's like a math puzzle.

HARVEST IS THE most *exciting* thing. Most of the year, I'm working by myself. Then harvest, I'm constantly working with people.

IT'S NIGHTTIME. You get to run around in the wee hours of the morning.

A 300- OR 350-FOOT-TALL redwood got struck by lightning and started on fire. Thank God Dad was close by. He had a dozer right above where the tree was.

QUITE A WAY to kick off harvest.

WHEN I DRIVE down the hill to Cazadero, I run into at least one person I know. We stop in the middle of the road and we chat.

THE MORE QUALITY you get, the more winemakers will want to make a vineyard-designate wine with your grapes.

IF YOU'RE GOING to grow grapes, why not grow darn good grapes and have it become amazing wine?

I DO FIND myself normally drinking a nice cold Coors.

INTERVIEWS

LESLIE WISER

FARMER

I FARM IN Sebastopol. The soil is just this beautiful sandy loam.

IT'S ABOUT AN acre and a half—not a very traditional farm. All 100-foot rows, with multiple plants, vegetables and herbs within the row.

I FIRST WANTED to be a farmer 20 years ago. I was interested in how food brings people together.

IN AN IMMIGRANT family, there are a lot of expectations about what success looks like.

YOU CAN BE a professional or start your own business. I did all of it. Now I want to do what I really want to do. That's how I'm starting a farm at 40.

MY CHINESE GRANDPARENTS were forced to flee to Taiwan. Never could go back. My mom came over from Taiwan when she was 24.

MY FATHER CAME over from Germany after World War II, when he was 10 years old.

I REMEMBER MY grandmother bemoaning that she couldn't get German and Polish ingredients. Sorrel and white asparagus, pastries, breads and meats.

THE FARM IS a project to repair that assimilation.

PEOPLE DON'T KNOW that Chinese laborers built a lot of the vineyards. And then anti-Chinese leagues popped up in Sonoma County to drive them out.

I EMAILED MY Chinese side and my German side and said, "What did you miss?" They sent me a list, and I put it all in the ground.

MY MOM LOVES my vegetables, but our customers aren't really her generation. People attracted to our farm are first- or second-generation kids of Asian descent.

WE INTERPLANT WITH marigolds, snap dragons and cosmos. So it's very colorful.

MY KIDS WERE the catalyst. I wanted to raise them on land.

INTERVIEWS

KYLE CONNAUGHTON

CHEF

THERE'S A JAPANESE expression which means "read the air." Understand, individually, the dynamics of each different guest, each table.

SINGLETHREAD IS A farm, a restaurant and a very small inn. Katina, my wife, runs our farm. We base everything we do around that.

THE "SINGLE THREAD" is hospitality.

GUESTS DON'T MAKE choices. It's based on what we're harvesting, and conversations about their dietary information, allergies, restrictions, all that.

WE'RE INSPIRED BY *omotenashi*, this Japanese idea of selflessly taking care of guests. We're less a "temple of cuisine" as a three-Michelin-star restaurant than we are focused on guests.

WE FIRST CAME to Healdsburg when we were 23. We just happened to stop on our way from getting married to Chez Panisse in Berkeley.

FROM THAT MOMENT to when we actually opened, it was 17 years.

KATINA and the farm team work on the produce for months. We have it in the kitchen for one day.

THIS IS WHAT'S best today. Yesterday was different. Tomorrow will be different. Which is a very Japanese thing as well: the fleeting moment of the present.

WE SEND EACH other lots of photos on Slack.

WE USE A Chinese and Japanese calendar that breaks down into five-day blocks. Things change quite rapidly.

THIS PEACH IS ready, this peach is not ready.

YESTERDAY WE WALKED by this persimmon tree that's going from light green to deep orange. I'm telling her about this new persimmon dessert we anticipate three weeks from now. That sense of excitement.

SHANNON SHAFFER-KILLEY

FIREFIGHTER

I JOINED THE Bodega Fire Department when I turned 18.

PEOPLE STILL HAVE this startled look: It's a weird thing, a female is driving a fire engine.

BODEGA PRETTY MUCH revolves around the fire department. We don't have a mayor or a town council. We have the fire department. That and the casino. Both my dad and my mom actually volunteered at one point.

EVEN IF YOU weren't a firefighter, you were still involved. Making desserts for events, helping set up, helping take down, creating a float for the parade.

BETWEEN 18 AND 20, I was super-focused on fire. I took an EMT course, a lot of different fire classes. Then I had my daughter and things shifted a bit, as they do.

A LOT OF times, it didn't cross my mind that I was the only girl out there until I was like, dude, I have to pee.

SOMEONE BRINGS you a five-pound paper bag with, like, 50,000 calories in it. You don't get to cook together, but you do eat together.

THE CAZADERO General Store makes its own jerky. They sent a volunteer up to the fire with a giant bag, and we were like, this is the best beef jerky ever.

I *HAD BEEN* almost 100 percent vegan.

THERE ARE AREAS we can't get to with our engines. A couple years back, we bought a Polaris—an ATV-type thing.

IT'S GOT A tank on it, chain saws, all sorts of stuff. We can do a lot with a little.

ON THE WALBRIDGE fire, they had us multiple places. Armstrong Woods, while it was still on fire, after it had burned through Bullfrog Pond.

ON MYERS GRADE, we let the fire burn literally to the ocean.

TONY COTURRI

WINEMAKER

I WAS CONSIDERED one of the most radical winemakers ever to live in California.

BUT MY WINE is completely conservative! I crush, ferment, put it in barrels, rack it a couple times and bottle it.

WHEN YOU'RE IN what's called "natural winemaking," you don't have a lot of options.

I'M A HIPPIE from the '60s. It was a time for getting rid of as much stuff as you can. Strip that thing down. Choppers were coming in for motorcycles. How much stuff can we take off this car?

MY ITALIAN GRANDFATHER lived in the Marina District in San Francisco. He was fermenting in a 60-gallon barrel. I remember opening the top—that very pungent smell of fermentation. I was about 10 years old.

I FACE THE Mayacamas Mountains. About an hour to the Golden Gate Bridge, about a quarter mile down a dirt road. My parents bought the property in 1961. I started making wine with my dad in 1963.

ONLY ITALIANS, Portuguese, Spanish and French drank wine. You were looked down on if you drank wine.

I HAD A private school for kids with learning disabilities for about seven years before I switched to full-time winemaking. I see those years as my community service.

IF I WENT into a wineshop talking about organic grapes, their eyes would glaze over. One shop was afraid the bottles would explode and spew biological contamination.

I QUICKLY LEARNED just to talk about the wine like everybody else. Once I made the sale, I'd say, "Oh, as an added attraction: natural yeast, organically grown."

IT MEANT I had to hone my craft to make wines that could

compete on the conventional level. They couldn't smell like barnyard. I had to make wines as good as anyone's or better—had to, to survive.

WE'RE AT A place now where a wine isn't a "natural wine" unless it has a problem.

I FIGURED OUT how to do a pét-nat cider with Gravenstein apples. I'm having a ball with it.

MONOCULTURE IS A huge problem. Even though apples are hardly a big diversification, at least it's something other than grapes.

THERE'S NO MONEY in the wine business unless you're Kendall-Jackson and you own property. It's a life question.

YOUR FACE IS in it. You get the aromas, the smells. You feel the hot spots and the cold spots.

INTERVIEWS

ARLEENE CORREA VALENCIA

ARTIST

MY YOUNGER SISTER started getting hives in East LA. The doctor basically said, "You have to move north."

I THINK ABOUT that a lot. How, as migrants, we end up in one place versus others.

MY UNCLES WOULD come home and pin grapes to the wall. "Wait. They're going to be yummy raisins."

THIS MAGICAL STORY: waiting for something to become sweet.

I LOVE WINE. Who grows up in Napa Valley who doesn't?

I REMEMBER BEING called wetback. Beaner. All these things that make you so afraid to reveal your history.

IN HONORS CLASSES, kids would ask if I knew how to read.

"I'M DONE. I'm going to community college. I'm doing art classes until I can figure something out."

A LOT OF harvesting happens at night. No visibility except for tractors carrying lights.

I LEAVE THE camera in the car, go straight into the fields and introduce myself.

AS SOON AS I speak Spanish, the barrier's broken. We talk about Michoacan: "I'm from 20 minutes north, or 20 minutes south."

IT'S LIKE, "OH, she wants to photograph me, I can be a painting." Everybody wants to be visible.

CARRYING 40 POUNDS of grapes above your head, running as fast as you can to keep up with the tractor.

BEING PART OF the night, being engraved into that smoky landscape. The reds and blues of wine that appear in the sky.

ALL THIS BEAUTY does not exist without the labor people put into it.

INTERVIEWS

ANDREW MARIANI

VINTNER

SCRIBE IS built on the shoulders of a lot of old Mariani farmers.

WHEN WE FIRST looked at this property, it had gotten pretty wild.

THERE WERE 15 turkey sheds. You had to take a series of chemical showers to get on the property. It was gnarly.

BUT BEHIND THAT, there was this house, all decrepit and beautiful and boarded up.

THIS HADN'T BEEN a viticultural property for almost 100 years. What happened pre-Prohibition was not on the surface.

WE KEPT discovering things. Old stone walls back in the ravine, covered with berry brambles.

THE DRESEL WINE Company is credited with the first riesling and sylvaner vines in America. These guys had done it here before. They'd done it for 70 vintages, and they were renowned.

WE FOUND AN old quote. Like an omen, from a book by Celeste G. Murphy. 1937. "Perhaps someday the spirit of the old generation will be recaptured and golden days of new triumph will return."

WE THOUGHT, let's tell that story: Old California and New California. It translates into how we make the wine, in a non-interventionist, transparent way.

I HAD POISON oak for a year.

MY GRANDFATHER was born in Yugoslavia—this island called Vis, part of Croatia now.

A LOT OF Yugoslavs moved to Santa Clara Valley. The story goes, the family got a tractor and rented it out. Made a little money, bought a little chunk of land. That grew and grew and grew.

FRUIT, NUTS, DRIED fruit. Almonds and walnuts.

MY GRANDFATHER CAME to the U.S. with nothing. The last

10 years of his life, he'd go to the restaurant he opened and eat a rack of lamb and drink a bottle of red wine every day.

SANTA CLARA slowly began to turn into Silicon Valley, and a lot of the family moved up north.

I WAS BORN in Winters. Small town, about 3,000 people.

I GREW UP driving forklifts, loading bins. You know one of the worst jobs? The water truck.

BLIGHT CAN HAPPEN if leaves get too dirty. They had a truck full of water to sprinkle on the roads.

I WAS 16. Four miles an hour down endless orchard roads. No radio. By the end of the summer, there was a lot of graffiti on the inside of that truck.

I WAS INTO music and art and writing. And wine somehow satisfied some of that, but was also farming.

SOME PEOPLE TALK about wine like it's on a pedestal. But this is farming. We're trying to transfer that into a bottle.

I'M OBSESSED WITH trying to glean energy out of the fruit.

MY BROTHER ADAM joined early on, after working on vineyards in Europe. And our sister Kelly, who's cooked in Italy and later at Chez Panisse, joined a few years after that. Now it's really a family.

WHEN YOU WALK through the Hacienda, you see these clues. Parts of the building are from the 1850s. You see renovations after the 1906 earthquake. You see 1950s boom renovations. ou can kind of walk through the history of California, right up to the present.

IT HARKENS BACK to this old California feeling of being wild and free out in the country.

ON A TYPICAL day, it feels busy. You want communal energy. This old house that sat vacant for years became a public place.

I'M CONSTANTLY popping things in my mouth. Taste fruit, stop in the garden, eat some leaves, stop by the kitchen, have a snack.

WHAT ARE WE saying? What do these bottles that we're pushing out into the world represent?

WINE IS JUST fruit. But it can give you this strange, mysterious feeling.

INTERVIEWS

ALEXANDRIA BROWN

HISTORIAN

I ALWAYS LIKE to push back on the idea that Napa's all wine.

A LOT OF fifth-generation, sixth-generation people—if you're raised there, you tend to stay there. I say that as somebody who moved back and forth multiple times.

THE CHINESE IN the 19th century, the Braceros in the 20th century—we would not have a Napa County if we didn't have those two groups.

OUR EARLIEST migrant laborers were Indigenous people. Then you get the Chinese, then Latinx people. You get Japanese people as well, then African Americans. Just a constant cycle: Which group can we pay the least to do the worst work?

IT'S NOT A pretty thing.

THE BRACERO PROGRAM was meant to replace American men who went off to World War II with Mexican men who could gain skills to bring back to Mexico.

THAT WAS THE intent. That's what was written on paper. Of course, white farmers exploited the hell out of that.

FROM ABOUT 1920 to about 1970, Napa's biggest agricultural product was actually cattle.

THERE WERE COWS everywhere, and we sold it all off and planted grapes. I remember watching that.

CALISTOGA AND ST. HELENA have a lot of rich people and a lot of poor people, and not a lot in between. But Napa was traditionally blue-collar and white-collar. Regular people.

WE DIDN'T HAVE keystone restaurants until the '70s.

I ALWAYS PITCH people on Pope Valley. Tourists never go up there. When I worked at the historical society, I'd tell people that if you want to see what Napa looked like before all the white folks showed up, go there.

INCLUDED

092 **SEASONS IN THE VALLEY**
By *Dorothy J. Gaiter*

098 **OSPREY TALKS TO ME ONE DAY**
By *Greg Sarris*

103 **FIREFALL**
By *Anne Goldman*

108 **CALIFORNIA'S VINTAGE VALE**
By *Frank Schoonmaker*

STORIES

Essays and selected writing from noted Napa and Sonoma voices

STORIES

SEASONS IN THE VALLEY

Written by **DOROTHY J. GAITER**

IN SUMMER 1975, my future husband, John, and I arrived in Napa Valley for the first time. We had taken Amtrak deluxe sleeper cars from Miami to San Francisco, with luggage bulging with Champagne bottles and long-stemmed glasses wrapped in our clothing, which we deemed so much more expendable. We rented a car in San Francisco and drove straight to Robert Mondavi Winery, domain of the man who had indirectly charmed us into the trip, the great winemaker and marketer Robert Mondavi. The renegade son of one of Napa's old-time immigrant families, he built Napa's first post-Prohibition winery in 1966. By '75, we'd tasted his wines and felt drawn to the source. John picked a grape from the vine nearest the iconic arched entrance that's pictured on the winery's labels.

We've visited wine regions all over the world, but Napa Valley and its calmer, more bucolic and sprawling neighbor to the west, Sonoma Valley, were like no places we'd visited. The mountains in Napa make it feel intimate, a sheltering environment for its dense concentration of vineyards. Sonoma is more expansive in its size and what it grows—from bustling poultry and dairy industries to heirloom Gravenstein apples that are feted with an annual fair—and, I've always thought, in the type of people who live there. Even before millionaires and billionaires invaded Napa, Sonoma was less precious. We wandered one day into the historic Hop Kiln winery [since sold] and interrupted a couple doing, well, what couples do behind closed doors.

We didn't know much about wine back then. We were hard-charging journalists at *The Miami Herald*. But we knew how to knock on doors, and in this new wine region, not yet discovered by hordes of tourists, we were greeted warmly everywhere by the winemaker himself—back then they were virtually all men—or by a family member. They were curious about us, too: an interracial couple enthusiastic enough about wine to travel clear across the country. We attended a Sonoma winegrowers' festival at Kenwood Vineyards, where we swooned over the wines and the smoked turkey. There was a drawing for prizes. We're pretty sure someone fixed it so we won a poster of the region's wineries that we still have.

"Luxury" had not fully arrived. The Sonoma Mission Inn was so minimalist that we could imagine it as a monastery. Our room, which we entered using a skeleton key, had hard twin beds.

We honeymooned in Napa in 1979, arriving by train as usual, and checked into the Harvest Inn in St. Helena. The inn was just 4 years old, small and nestled in vineyards. Back then, Beaulieu Vineyard sold a few bottles of the famous 1968 and 1974 Georges de Latour Private Reserve cabernet sauvignon for $35 each. These wines were so cherished that even famous winemakers stood in line to purchase them at the winery, one per customer. Like eminent Bordeaux from France, these wines had classic structure and elegance, but they were made with adroitly harnessed, rich California fruit. The combination of Old World winemaking and New World bold fruit made them benchmarks for American cabernet sauvignon. And with good reason: They were crafted by Russian emigré André Tchelistcheff, who influenced three generations of winemakers by the time he died, in 1994, a few years after we met him.

We bought the last '68 that day, asked our innkeeper for glasses, walked straight into the vineyard and drank that wine as the sun set over the mountains. Leaning into each other for warmth as the cooling winds that grapes love so much swept down into the valley, we agreed that it was the greatest wine we'd ever had.

The area's small-town-that-time-forgot vibe began changing after news of a hardly noticed but nonetheless momentous event had sunk in. In 1976, in a four-paragraph article in *Time* magazine that bore no byline, this was reported: Two Napa Valley wines had beaten famous French wines in a blind tasting called "the Judgement of Paris." The win by Warren Winiarski's Stag's Leap Cellars cabernet sauvignon and a 1973 Chateau Montelena chardonnay made by Mike Grgich announced the arrival of California's wine industry. The moment also gave winemakers worldwide the confidence that they, too, could make wines of excellence far from the French heartland.

A seismic shift began. It took some time, as America still wasn't the wine-drinking nation it is today. Tourism began to grow in what became known as California Wine Country, though I can't remember ever seeing another Black person in those days—not as guests in the inns, or in the kitchens, or tending the vines. But big money, corporate and private, from the U.S. and abroad, followed the breakthrough.

While we always have a wonderful time there, wine country is far from perfect, despite how it looks. We're nostalgic for the time before the advent of tasting fees that with few exceptions have gotten out of hand, especially in Napa. A time before wineries started employing people more intent on selling wine club memberships than whether you actually like what they're pouring. Before tourist traffic—clogged roads led to wineries open now "by appointment only," and before big wineries started gobbling up smaller ones. That austere mission inn is now the posh Fairmont Sonoma Mission Inn & Spa.

Although Winiarski and others won passage in 1968 of the Napa Agricultural Preserve, reserving thousands of acres for agricultural or open-land use, residents still battle endlessly about development— especially how to protect water sources, given perennial wildfires. And lack of diversity remains a problem. Three decades after our first visit, while on assignment for "Tastings," the wine column John and I created in 1998 for *The Wall Street Journal*'s new Weekend edition, we dropped in on a winery in Napa on busy Highway 29. The tasting room attendant glanced up with a big smile and said, "You two back so soon?" That's when we knew there was another interracial couple in the valley.

***

February 2020. We were at Copia—formally the Culinary Institute of America at Copia: The American Center for Wine, Food and the Arts, a dream of Robert Mondavi. The University of California, Davis, home to what's been called "the greatest wine library in the world," was celebrating our donation of materials related to "Tastings." Those papers, from the nearly 12-year run of the column, include notes, art, memorabilia and videos from TV appearances. There's also an American flag flown in combat over Afghanistan in 2008, sent to us by a fan in the Air Force. That night at Copia, a computer screen displayed the *Jeopardy!* question from 2005 about Open That Bottle Night [OTBN], the annual worldwide celebration of wine and friendship that John and I invented. OTBN falls on the last Saturday in February. That happened to be this night.

It was a night that made clear the linkage between past and future

in wine country. Our papers are part of the UC Davis Library's Warren Winiarski Wine Writer Collection, and Winiarski himself was there, in his 90s, joyfully overseeing the celebration. There were guests from our years of writing "Tastings," when there were virtually no Black people, to speak of, in any facet of the industry. There, too, were Black people and Brown people we've met more recently while writing for *Grape Collective*, an online magazine with a wine store in Manhattan, where we now live. The inclusion of ethnic and racial minorities in the industry is a necessity if it is to thrive.

In the audience were Ernie Weir, whose Hagafen Cellars makes fine kosher wines that hit our lists of favorites, and Cam and Kate Solari Baker of Larkmead Vineyards, who funded online discussions in 2020 about the industry's future at a time of great uncertainty. Theodora Lee, a Black trial lawyer who owns Theopolis Vineyards in Mendocino, dropped in. Rolando and Lorena Herrera were there, too. Winiarski met Herrera when the young man from Mexico was a teenager. To make extra money, Rolando took a job breaking rocks for a wall near Stag's Leap Cellars, which Winiarski sold in 2007. In 1997, he founded his Napa winery, Mi Sueño, "My Dream," which has encouraged other Hispanics to pursue careers in wine.

As late as 2020, there was still only one Black-owned estate winery in Napa Valley, Brown Estate. In Sonoma, there are a few wineries founded and owned by Black winemakers, including Vision Cellars, Bodkin Wines and L'Objet Noir. Carlton McCoy, at the time one of only three Black master sommeliers in the world and since 2018 the president and CEO of legendary Heitz Cellars, was there, too, as was Kevin Zraly, whose Windows on the World wine course and books have educated millions and who himself launched the careers of many influential wine people.

When our talk ended, we took in a surprising sight, especially for Napa: a queue of Black women, there, serendipitously, for a conference on women in wine. Women like Julia Coney, who after police killed George Floyd in Minneapolis three months later, began assembling the Black Wine Professionals list to silence the go-to excuse of "I can't hire them if I don't know who they are." J'nai Gaither, who brought her mother to meet me, later penned a moving piece, "What Racism Looks Like Inside a Napa Valley Tasting Room."

I felt maternal, grateful to witness this nascent wave of young Black wine professionals. After much hugging and picture-taking—this was just before 2020's time of social distancing and lockdowns—about 40 of us retreated to a private dining room. McCoy, a sweet and generous transplant from Aspen, produced a 1968 Beaulieu Vineyard Georges de Latour Private Reserve cabernet sauvignon, the wine from our honeymoon.

That wine was a rose-scented dowager, with a beneficent core of fruit and earth, confident in the wisdom it had gained over the years. It had weathered a lot but, like Napa and Sonoma, was still breathtakingly beautiful.

DOROTY J. GAITER is senior editor of *Grape Collective*, an online wine magazine. With her husband, John Brecher, she conceived and wrote *The Wall Street Journal*'s wine column for 12 years and co-authored four wine books. She has had a distinguished career as a reporter, editor, columnist and editorial writer at *The Miami Herald* and *The New York Times* as well as at *The Wall Street Journal*.

OSPREY TALKS TO ME ONE DAY

Written by **GREG SARRIS**

REMEMBER A PLACE along the river. Recall the season, the time of day, how the sun shone on the water, the trees' shadows. Wohler Bridge. 1972. Midsummer. Midday. On a sandy beach where the river bends just before meeting the bridge. I am 10 years old, alone. Clear water ripples like beveled glass; small fish, no doubt carp, tease and dart at the shore. But what's caught my attention is a single silver osprey, a bird I've noticed coursing the river countless times before, hovering now midair above me.

On weekends sunbathers, mostly young, carve out spots, a patch of sand, maybe under a shady willow, to drink beer and smoke weed. And, yes, to swim naked. They park in an empty lot below the bridge and hike north. But I knew of this place long before, when, as an even younger man, I accompanied Pomo basket-maker and medicine woman Mabel McKay to pick herbs and cut willow branches for basket-making. I remember paper bags filled with Mountain Balm, for asthma Mabel said, and I can still see the armfuls of straight willow branches tied with strips of colored cloth that we hauled back to her car parked under a redwood near the bridge. Mabel was a Lake County Pomo. It was her good friend Essie Parrish, a medicine woman like Mabel, who first told her of the place. Essie Parrish, a Kashaya or Southwestern Pomo, like others of her generation from Southern Pomo tribes, knew the Russian River well, its nooks and crannies, where to fish, where to gather herbs. "Medicine growing," Mabel called the place, perhaps using Essie's name for it.

The Indigenous people did not think of the river as a 110-mile body of water as a geographer might. They didn't conceive of it as a single unit or phenomenon, but rather as a continuum of interconnected places, no different from the way they understand all features of the wider landscape, each with its own character and story. The storied landscape thus is a sacred text, an outcropping of rocks, a mountain peak, the river mouth, all mnemonic pegs not only reminding us of the world we find ourselves in but how to live harmoniously with it. Except for the Coast Miwok, located south of the river, the Indigenous nations are Pomo. Both terms—Coast Miwok and Pomo—are linguistic classifications. We never referred to ourselves as such. We belonged to at least a dozen distinct nations, identified by the boundaries of our respective territories. Sometimes a central village name identified a nation's people. "Peta · luma." Sloping ridge. The Kashaya Pomo called the river near present-day Jenner "Shabaiki," or south water place. One Southern Pomo nation referred to a place near present-day Healdsburg as "Ashokawa," east water place. Often a feature of the landscape was used, as in the case of "Peta luma." Other locals were associated with fish and animals. Coho Salmon House. Grizzly Bear Path. Rattlesnake Coming Out.

Villages, indeed entire nations, were organized and located around bodies of water. Creeks. Lakes. The Santa Rosa Lagoon. The Russian River. Each nation was responsible for the health of its water. Willows had to be cut back, lest falling branches clog the water, impede its flow. Sedge was maintained for the same reason. Since all bodies of water connect to one another, throughout the territory of at least 12 distinct independent nations each with 500 to 2,000 individuals, the health of the water was indicative of the well-being between nations. If nations in the foothills did not take care of their creeks, ensuring clean, free-flowing water for migrating fish to spawn, the nations located near river marshes forbade them to dig for water potatoes that grew in the marshes. Likewise if the marsh reeds and river trails were neglected, the hill nations wouldn't trade for herbs and flint for arrow making found only in the hills. Dozens of large creeks join the river, including the Maacama Creek east of Healdsburg, along which numerous Indigenous villages were located. A healthy river meant peace.

In a clean river fish were abundant. Steelhead. Salmon. White sturgeon. Stories of spawning salmon so thick at the mouth of the river that a person could cross to the other side on their shiny black backs. There were white sturgeon the size of small whales. Porpoises frolicked up river as far inland as Guerneville. Mostly people fished with nets. "Get your nets ready," tribal leaders would call as the fish began to migrate upstream. There were abundant animals too, beavers

STORIES

and sea otters, not seen today or rarely. Seals always camped on the river shore near the ocean, competing with people and grizzly bears for fish, especially salmon. Oh, and there are so many stories … Near Jenner a young Pomo was leaching acorns in the sand. Busy talking to another woman also leaching acorns, she'd lost track of her young son. He'd found his way upriver, not too far from his mother but out of her sight—this was on the north side of the river where today cattle graze on green grass that meets the water. Startled, she found the boy, and saw a huge white sturgeon head out of the water appearing ready to swallow the boy from the shore. Luckily, she reached him in time. But then, not long after she got home [she left her acorn meal in the sand], her son fell into a coma. The villagers were living on a ranch, tending sheep and cattle for a white man. When the medicine man came in from work, he prayed over the boy. "What did you see?" the medicine man asked the boy when he woke. "An old man in the river," the boy answered. "He told me he was lonely for his people. There weren't many left." "Yes," the medicine man said. He turned to the boy's mother. "He didn't want to eat your son. He was telling him that he can't forget his people. What happened to the fish can happen to us too."

My family traces its history to the river. As Indigenous people in Sonoma and Mendocino counties, we all do. My great-great-great-grandmother Tsupu [baptized Maria Checca] was born near Peta · luma, sloping ridge. Her father was born in a village on Mark West Creek, which joins the Russian River north of Forestville. Her son, Tom Smith, the last Coast Miwok medicine man, built a ceremonial Roundhouse on the Jenner Head. There he preached about the importance of remembering our traditions, the rules of living with the land. Pointing to the river, he said, "Like that water, we are connected to everything. It's memory."

His granddaughter, my grandmother, sat below the redwoods at Wohler Bridge watching cockfights with her friends and relatives. Filipino farmworkers, the *manongs*, hosted the fights. A large bonfire was built. They wore their best clothes—pinstriped suits, gold chains, Panama hats—never mind the spurting blood, mostly to impress the single Indian girls gathered for the fight. An anti-miscegenation law forbade a Filipino man a marriage license in California at the time, and American Indians were some of the only women available to these young bachelors brought from the Philippines to work on farms and in kitchens. Today, there is a significant amount of Filipino ancestry in the tribes. My grandmother lived in Los Angeles after she married my Filipino grandfather in 1929 [in Tijuana, so she would have a marriage license], but she returned with him to visit family and friends, and one of the best places to find them was at the Wohler Bridge cockfights, located, coincidentally, where I parked my car before heading up the river to swim.

In 1972, I didn't know about the cockfights. I would learn about them from my grandfather and other manongs. My grandmother, whom I didn't know, comes alive in a story. I see her by the bonfire, roosters at each other midair, just as I see, from another story, a small Indian boy, and hardly a foot away, the face of a fish large as a whale. I see salmon plentiful enough that I can walk across them like a bridge. I see sea otters wrestling on a muddy shore, and beaver dams the size of houses atop the water. I see clean water ... and me now. 1972. Wohler Bridge. A warm summer day. I start to peel off my clothes to swim. But then I stop, looking back up at the magnificent silver bird still hovering above me. "I know the river," the bird says. "Follow me," and already I'm in the sky able to see below me the length of the river and a hundred places I can land.

GREG SARRIS has published several books, including *Grand Avenue*, an award-winning collection of short stories. He is serving his 14th elected term as chairman of the Federated Indians of Graton Rancheria and teaches at Sonoma State University. This essay also appears in the collection *The Russian River and Its Watershed*, from Santa Rosa's Riparianthology Press, featuring art by Richard McDaniel.

FIREFALL

Written by **ANNE GOLDMAN**

THE DAY AFTER I MOVED into a cabin in Sebastopol, I fled. For years, I had wished myself into a place like this one, hoping I might eventually wake up as well as work in Sonoma, where grapevines contour hills in landscapes Dürer could have etched. But the date I started my tenancy proved turbulent. Even as the movers carted in my possessions, Diablo winds skittering above the slopes of the Sierras began to hurl themselves across a bone-dry Central Valley. After gaining heat and hurricane speeds, these fierce disturbances swept into San Francisco. While I surveyed the sprawl of my things, wind was scudding across Bodega Bay and wrinkling the water by Doran Beach into shivering silver. At the roadside fish houses, furnace-like gusts wrenched plates away from people dipping crabmeat into cocktail sauce. Up the coast at Furlong Gulch, gulls strove against the jagged vectors of air flinging them toward rocks, regaining altitude before parting from one another like Thunderbird planes.

As I unwrapped a glass sheathed in newsprint, an emergency alert lit up the phone and began to shriek its drone and pause and repeat. Friends and colleagues had lost houses in blazes, yet I froze in disbelief.

Fire and fall have always been twined in California, but the changing climate has made them inseparable. Still, it is one thing to recall Joan Didion's sentences about the Santa Anas that bring chaos to the Los Angeles mountains and another to watch smoke fill your own atmosphere. In the rambling garden in back of the cottage I had just leased, wind pummeled a Chinese scholar tree until its tasseled yellow foliage blurred into liquid gold leaf. Just beyond the windows that usher the outside into this compact building, a pyracantha bush loaded with crimson berries swayed left, danced right and bowed sideways.

Lodged tight in boxes, my books stayed put and my ceramics held fast. But my heart beat fast, too, stumbling over its rhythm so that I could not think what to take with me. The phrases scrawled on the sides of the cardboard towers massed in the living room did not help. Should I drag out the photo albums from the nearest column, or hurry back and forth ferrying paintings from bedroom to doorway?

Unable to decide, I jerked an unpacked suitcase upright, grabbed my wallet and hoisted a tote bag heavy with books onto one shoulder. Outside, the sky was slate, and the smell of burning wood—part acrid and part earthy—was strong. A trace of vinegar laced the air: grapes sizzling in a vineyard.

> **AT THE ROADSIDE FISH HOUSES, FURNACE-LIKE GUSTS WRENCHED PLATES AWAY FROM PEOPLE DIPPING CRABMEAT INTO COCKTAIL SAUCE.**

Fine gray grit sleeted the car's dashboard. Plants and trees rustled and creaked. The pulse sounding in my ear beat loudly over all of them, quicker than the tick-tick-tick of a clock. I drove away without even throwing water over the fireglow maple my brother had planted for me in a wide blue pot whose leaves had long since exchanged spring's blood-red tints for green.

"Nature's first green is gold / Her hardest hue to hold," Robert Frost begins in "Nothing Gold Can Stay," one of many poems that juxtapose the straight lines of our life spans with the cycles of seasons. Though Frost was born in San Francisco, his work, like his name, evokes New England's icy winters more frequently than its transient summers, whose midpoint, the "singer" in "The Oven Bird" tells us, remains as far from spring as "one to ten." The landscapes Frost creates, like the phrases reeled out by Walt Whitman and the lines that hang in the air of Emily Dickinson's poems, build the language of weather readers recognize from coast to coast. But when it comes to seasonal time, Northern Californians are out of sync with the nation as a whole. We share a Mediterranean climate with just six sites on the globe: the shores of the Med basin and five small areas in the Southern Hemisphere. In Sonoma, as elsewhere by the California coast, winter is a sodden relief. Then rain beats down upon hills summer has long since bleached to tawny hues that bristle like the flanks of sleeping cows.

And still, I yearn for fall. Autumn is ardent. Fading chlorophyll spells the extinction of leaves, but just as some dying minds are illumined by a synaptic storm for a few seconds before they go dark, the trees bloom brightest in the weeks before they reduce themselves to skeletons. In the mountains east of Sebastopol, trees take on hues beyond the art of Renaissance masters to mix. In September and October, the anthocyanins that pigment blueberries and plums announce themselves in dogwoods and sumac, while the carotenoids that yellow daffodils and brighten pumpkins bronze ginkgoes and turn aspens into sparklers.

In fall, masses of crimson float above lakes from the Catskills to California. Our hearts burn along with them—until fire makes trees writhe. As strips of eucalyptus bark curl and shrink, our skin grows clammy. Soon, orange enrobes the forest. In the end, what could pass for monochrome poles stake out vast swaths of smoking ground that mark where houses and forests used to be.

But nowhere are the hazards and plenitude of the harvest more closely interwoven than in counties like Sonoma. By September, the fruit trees that line street after street are laden. Figs hang from branches, while other trees become englobed with the mottled red and green Gravensteins that lend their name to the highway winding through the West County's apple orchards. Ripening pomegranates bejewel the front yards of some of my neighbors. In others, sunflowers vie with corn in front of Japanese maples whose leaves will shift from the colors of squash and flamingos before deepening to the burgundy fermenting in wine cellars only a few miles away.

Two days before Halloween, in 2019, I turned my car back toward the home I had evacuated a week earlier. As I set my cottage to rights, crows chattered in their separate voices and crickets took over the nights. Two weeks later, the rain came in sheets, tossing the solar lights I hung in the branches of the shrubs beyond the window like shipboard beacons on stormy seas.

A year later, I write in the interim before winter sets in. Some evenings, I pour ruby or gold into a half-full glass and sit turned toward trees on the verge of brilliance. Flocks of cedar waxwings devour berries beginning to ferment. Sometimes they hit the windows with a thud, mistaking glass for the air through which they wing. One day, for 10 long minutes, a bird with a bandit mask sits stuporous after dashing itself against the pane. Its breast heaves, revealing the single red stripe that seems to answer the carmine berries from which it sipped.

I walk out into the somnolence of late afternoon. The trees are quiet, but a few straw-colored grasses rustle as if they would pick themselves up and leave their places. Slowly, the street falls toward the Laguna flatlands. At the head of the trail, I take in the soft blue of the encircling mountains. Swallows crisscross the sky, quick as bats. The path curves and I am face-to-face with the cows of the neighboring dairy. For a reason of their own, they have gathered near the mesh that fences them in the broad field that adjoins this pathway. Moving deliberately as a metal crane, one swivels its neck toward me. Silence. For a moment, nothing moves but the flies that mascara its eye. Then my own are caught by a rarity. A flame-colored monarch sieves currents too slight for me to sense. It hovers and dips and rises. Then, flimsy as a scrap of scorched paper, it drifts out of sight.

ANNE GOLDMAN is the author of *Stargazing in the Atomic Age: Essays*. Her work has appeared in *Tin House*, *The Guardian*, *The Georgia Review*, *The Gettysburg Review* and elsewhere and has been cited in *The Best American Travel Writing*, *The Best American Science and Nature Writing*, and *The Best American Essays*. She teaches at Sonoma State University.

STORIES

CALIFORNIA'S VINTAGE VALE

Written by **FRANK SCHOONMAKER**

IN A COUNTRY WHERE SUPERLATIVES FLY in flocks, like migrating birds, where it is possible to drive through a tree rather than around it or into it, where the mountains are 14,000 feet high and where the climate—in other words, in California—the Napa Valley is in a class by itself. It is not spectacular; it is not even very big. Its "natural wonders," which include a modest petrified forest and a few friendly pint-size geysers, are not very wonderful. It is a little over an hour's drive from San Francisco and you can see it easily in a day. Then why, you may say, why Napa?

Some twenty-five years ago Sidney Howard wrote a most engaging comedy about the troubles of a Napa Valley winegrower—*They Knew What They Wanted*. This was later made into an excellent movie, starring Charles Laughton, and was at least partially filmed in the valley near St. Helena. If, at some future date, the powers that be in Napa County decide to adopt a motto for their great seal, I would strongly counsel them to forget the usual highfalutin Latin and adopt, with a bow to Mr. Howard, "We Knew What We Wanted." For they did. And they do. And they have it.

More than once I have sat in the warm fragrant dusk of the California summer, on a terrace overlooking the hillside vineyards, a bottle of cool Napa wine at my elbow, and the lights of San Francisco and Oakland turning the southern horizon into a sort of man-made aurora borealis, and wondered why anyone who had seen the Napa Valley ever lived anyplace else.

This is one of those few fortunate corners of the world where contentment and quiet seem almost part of the air one breathes. Yet Napa's tranquility is of a rather special sort—it is no Shangri-La. The busy world is at its doorstep, and if it seems like a transplanted bit of Northern Italy or France, it has fully as much of the old California in the pattern of its life.

Perhaps this is due to Napa's vineyards and her wine. People who grow grapes and make wine, the world over, seem to have a particularly relaxed attitude toward life, and Napa, with her sister counties Sonoma and Santa Clara, is the heart and kernel of America's fine-wine country—our own native counterpart of Bordeaux and Burgundy and the Rhineland. In the narrow Napa Valley alone there are over 15,000 acres planted to wine grapes; the per capita consumption of red and white table wine is probably higher here than in any other county in the United States, and the whole valley is dotted with impressive and venerable stone wineries where Napa wines are stored while they acquire age and polish in cool darkness and silence.

Although perhaps at its best at vintage time, in September, the Napa Valley is lovely the year round. Mount St. Helena, which rears its great bald crest more than 4,000 feet at the valley's northern end, is often snow-covered in winter, but oranges and grapefruit flourish in the more sheltered corners of the valley floor. By late February the vineyards are a yellow carpet of wild mustard, soon to be plowed under, and the gardens are golden with mimosa and noisy with birds. It is fairly hot in summer and, strangely, the northern end of the valley is much warmer than the southern, but there is almost always a cool breeze off San Francisco Bay at night.

Still, Napa's real season is the early autumn. As the grapes begin to ripen, toward the end of August, the pastureland and hills are already parched and brown, but the vines are green, and there is an excitement in the air. Preparations are already being made, in St. Helena, for the vintage festival, which takes place after the harvest, usually the last week end of September. This is a charming fiesta, with costumes and dances, and for the two or three days it lasts all of the wineries in the valley have open house.

Meanwhile, in the little bars and taverns of the valley towns—Oakville, Rutherford, St. Helena, Calistoga—you will find men talking the special argot of the cellar and vineyard. Jerry Draper's Rieslings on Spring Mountain have shown 16 Balling; the Cabernets on the Tokalon Ranch, as a result of the spring rains, have more than their share of shot berries; there is mildew in the Folle Blanche around Oakville; the Inglenook Pinots will run under a ton and a half per acre this year—and much more in this vein. This special lingo is vastly interesting if you can understand it, for it has to do with the quality of the wine you will be serving on your dining-room table a few years from now.

***

The life of the valley—its business and its hobby, its study and its profession, its first love and its last—is wine. The devotees [and very jolly, hospitable devotees they are] include Frenchmen, Italians, Germans, a Russian or two, some Scots, Texans, New Englanders, native sons. Among them are the young and the old, the talkative and the quiet, the excitable and the calm, the boastful and the modest, the shrewd and the impractical. All have one thing in common: an abiding interest in wine, and a passion for it.

Talk to Lee Stewart. His Souverain Cellars winery is a little old stone structure built into a hillside high above St. Helena; the oak puncheons in which its wines are stored are polished until they shine; from the open space in front of the building and from the Stewart house a few feet away, you can see the whole Napa Valley spread out at your feet like a wonderfully colored map. Souverain has won medals for its Zinfandel, its Pinot Noir, its Vin Rosé.

"Taste this," says Lee. And then, almost aggressively, "It's not for sale. But what variety of grape do you think it's made from?"

And when the wine has been carefully sniffed, considered, discussed, almost dissected, and emerges finally as a Johannisberg Riesling, made from a grape of celebrated ancestry transplanted from the Rhine Valley, the nods and smiles and congratulations go round.

Lee Stewart is not a rich man. But I doubt whether, if he were a captain of industry with a floor in Rockefeller Center for his office, he would find life as good.

Talk to my charming old friend Mr. Ballantine. He is cursed with arthritis and blessed with a good-looking, intelligent and attentive son. For some thirty years he was coachman for Mrs. Tobin Clark of Burlingame, just south of San Francisco. His winery is the love and delight of his retirement, and he knows wine and relishes it as most of his compatriots from north of the Tweed love the whisky of their native heath. Lately he has found a volcanic spring, high on the mountain, whose waters he claims have done wonders for him; but nothing, not even the miraculous spring, will ever bring quite the light to his eyes and the smile to his face as your enthusiastic "Wonderful" when he has brought you "*a veery special* Sylvaner" from one of the hill vineyards around his stone winery and upland home. He is an artisan and a good one, and proud of his work, as indeed he should be.

Talk to Bob Mondavi. He and his brother own and run the historic Charles Krug winery just north of St. Helena. The enormous live oaks in his yard are four times Bob's age, and the massive winery is far older than his father and perhaps his grandfather. Bob and his brother, being young, are full of new ideas, bubbling over with the result of experiments they have made in the early bottling of white wines, as practiced in Germany, and the aging of red wines in small cooperage, as practiced in France. The impressive array of medals in their tasting room is eloquent proof that their pioneering is not in vain.

"Tell me," Bob will say, in a voice that cracks a little when he is excited, "do you think we will ever make in California a better Traminer than this?" The wine is pale, fresh, with a wonderful flavor of the true Traminer grape.

"Well, maybe, but not soon, and perhaps not in our lifetime." And Bob is happy.

Or talk to John Daniel. As you drive up the main valley road toward St. Helena, you come to what might be called, not a village, but an excuse for a village, named Rutherford. Against the hills to the left, there is a mile-wide foreground of perfectly tended vines, and a vast old stone winery outlined against one of the foothills. Inglenook.

It was founded by a famous old Finnish fur trader who made a fortune in Alaska when still a young man, and chose Inglenook as the place to spend his declining years. John Daniel is his descendant and also a key officer in the major associations which govern California wine affairs.

I met John Daniel for the first time at a memorable dinner at the Bohemian Club in San Francisco, nearly fifteen years ago. I was a newcomer to California and before my astonished eyes and upon my astonished palate came forth a series of wonders—Inglenook Cabernets dating from 1900, still vigorous and fine, and a whole collection of other Inglenook wines which had somehow survived Prohibition in John Daniel's private cellar.

Reminded of such past glories, John will say, with his quiet smile, "We are doing even better now."

***

As you visit the wineries of Napa and talk to their owners and to those who have devoted their lives to winemaking, you begin to note certain names, perhaps unfamiliar names, cropping up again and again in their talk. Cabernet, Cabernet, Cabernet. Much talk of various grapes called Pinot and pronounced *P-no*, of Riesling, pronounced *Ree-sling*, not *Rye-sling*, of Zinfandel, Traminer, Sylvaner, Gamay and a half dozen others. They are worth remembering, for they are part of the vocabulary of anyone who knows California wines—or those of Europe too.

These are names of different varieties of wine grape; a careful winemaker would no more use a raisin grape or a table grape than a dog breeder would enter a French poodle or a great Dane in a field trial. And as in kennel-club shows, the champions among wine grapes are always those thoroughbreds of established origin and bloodstream, which run true to type and class. The best California producers, including, of course, those of Napa, invariably put a grape name on their best bottles—the name of the grape out of which the wine was made. And a rigid Government control effectively prevents falsification.

There are other things you will learn in Napa—that fine wine grapes cannot be grown just anywhere; they require a special combination of temperate climate and not-too-fertile soil. That hillside vineyards are the best—the poet Virgil was right when he said, two thousand years ago, that "Bacchus loves the hillsides." You will learn, too, that there is as much of science as of tradition in the making of fine wine. The larger producers now have their own laboratories; the great Pasteur himself owed much of his early reputation to the study of wine yeasts and fermentation.

You will begin to feel, in Napa, the fascination that the subject of wine has had for people of all kinds and for centuries on end. Literally thousands of books have been written about wine but no one has said the last word, and no one ever will. Why is the wine from one hillside markedly better than that from another hillside, a mile away? Why does a wine age more rapidly in a small barrel than a large one, and why is it happier in oak than in any other wood? Why does a wine from one grape mature and mellow in a single year while a wine from another, very similar grape takes five years to "come round"? Why do some wines taste better when they are chilled, and others at the temperature of the cellar or the dining room?

We do not know the answers to these questions but we have our opinions and talk about them, and that, too, is part of the fun.

Finally, you will, or should, learn in Napa that you do not need a rule book, a service chart and a vintage table to enjoy good wine, despite what many self-styled connoisseurs will tell you. It is almost as easy to tell good wine from bad as good beef from poor, and you do not have to be an expert to like the good.

Wine, as they know in Napa, goes with good company and good food. It is at home in Napa and Napa, thanks to wine, is in the best sense a Happy Valley.

Prosperous and easygoing, an odd and charming combination of the old world and the new, isolated, yet almost within sight of San Francisco's white, sunlit skyscrapers and her great modern bridges, the Napa Valley is unique. Not breathtaking, not spectacular, not magnificent. But as you head southward along the highway, with Napa behind you and the Pacific to your right, you will look back reluctantly and say to yourself, as a great many people have said before you, "One of these days I'm coming back to Napa." And you will.

FRANK SCHOONMAKER (1905-1976) was a South Dakota-born wine aficionado, entrepreneur and travel writer. He is the author of numerous books (including *Through Europe on Two Dollars a Day*) and magazine articles. During World War II, Schoonmaker served as an Office of Strategic Services operative in Madrid and France; shortly thereafter, he reported to *The New Yorker* regarding the wines of occupied Germany. This piece appeared in the revered travel journal *Holiday* in 1952.

DIRECTORY & INDEX

WINE DIRECTORY

WINERIES/VINEYARDS

Ashes & Diamonds Winery *Napa*
Aperture Cellars *Healdsburg*
Beaulieu Vineyard *Rutherford*
Bodkin Wines *Healdsburg*
Brown Estate *Napa*
Buena Vista Vineyard *Sonoma*
Ceja Vineyards *Sonoma*
Charles Krug Winery *St Helena*
Chateau Montelena Winery *Calistoga*
Checkerboard Vineyards *Calistoga*
Cobb Wines *Occidental*
Corison Winery *St Helena*
Coturri Winery *Glen Ellen*
Dehlinger Winery *Sebastopol*
Del Dotto's Vineyards *St Helena*
DeLoach Vineyards *Santa Rosa*
Dirty & Rowdy Family Winery *Napa*
Donelan Family Wines *Santa Rosa*
Drinkward Peschon *St Helena*
Elyse Winery *Napa*
Enfield Wine Co *Napa*
Etude *Napa*
Far Niente Winery *Oakville*
Flowers Vineyards & Winery *Healdsburg*
Francis Ford Coppola Winery *Geyserville*
Frog's Leap *Rutherford*
Girard Winery *Yountville*
Guerrero Fernandez Winery *Windsor*
Gundlach Bundschu Winery *Sonoma*
Hagafen Cellars *Silverado Trail*
Hall Wines *St Helena*
Harvest Moon Estate & Winery *Santa Rosa*
Heitz Cellar *St Helena*
Hellenthal Vineyard *Cazadero*
Hirsch Vineyards *Healdsburg*
Hook & Ladder Winery *Santa Rosa*
Hudson Ranch & Vineyards *Napa*
Inglenook *Rutherford*
Iron Horse Vineyards *Sebastopol*

Jessup Cellars *Yountville*
Jolie-Laide *Sebastopol*
Joseph Phelps Vineyards *St Helena*
Kendall-Jackson *Santa Rosa*
La Sirena *Calistoga*
Larkmead Vineyards *Calistoga*
L'Objet Wines *Healdsburg*
Marcassin Vineyard *Windsor*
Martha Stoumen Wines *Sebastopol*
Massican Winery *St Helena*
Matthiasson Winery *Napa*
Mi Sueño *Napa*
Mount Veeder Winery *Rutherford*
Nichelini Family Winery *St Helena*
Odette Estate Winery *Napa*
Outland *Napa*
Peay Vineyards *Cloverdale*
Poe Wines *Napa*
Priest Ranch *Yountville*
Reeve Wines *Healdsburg*
Ridge Vineyards *Healdsburg*
Robert Mondavi Winery *Oakville*
Robert Sinskey Vineyards *Napa*
Schramsberg Vineyards *Calistoga*
Screaming Eagle *Oakville*
Scribe Winery *Sonoma*
Seghesio Family Vineyards *Healdsburg*
Sky Vineyards *Glen Ellen*
Somerston Estate *Yountville*
St Clair Brown Winery *Napa*
Stags' Leap Winery *Yountville*
Stewart Cellars *Yountville*
Stony Hill Vineyard *St Helena*
Tank Garage Winery *Calistoga*
The Terraces *Rutherford*
Trefethen Family Vineyards *Napa*
Turley Wine Cellars *St Helena*
Valdez Family Winery *Cloverdale*
Vision Cellars *Sonoma County*

WINESHOPS

Abbot's Passage *Sonoma*
Acme Fine Wines *St Helena*
Arlequin *San Francisco*
Bacchus & Venus *Sausalito*
Backroom Wines *Napa*
Bay Grape Wine *Oakland*
Bottle Barn *Santa Rosa*
Cadet *Napa*
Castro Village *San Francisco*
Compline *Napa*

Dick Warner Wines *Petaluma*
Farmstead *Alameda*
Fatted Calf *Napa*
Gary's Wine *St Helena*
Joseph George *San Jose*
Mendocino Country Store
Minimo *Oakland*
Miracle Plum *Santa Rosa*
Oakland Yard *Oakland*
Ordinaire *Oakland*

Outland *Napa*
Oxbow *Napa*
Redwood *Sebastopol*
Region *Sebastopol*
Ruby *San Francisco*
Sonoma Wine Shop *Sonoma*
Terroir *San Francisco*
Vino Locale *Palo Alto*
Vintage Berkeley *Berkeley*
William Cross *San Francisco*

INDEX

Abbott, Bette 23
Acre Coffee 29
Ad Hoc 17
Alien Land Law 51
Alma's Oil Cloth and Chucherias 21
Already Dead 12
American Viticultural Areas 34
Angela Channing 46
Anti-Chinese bigotry 51
Aperture Estate 9
Ashes & Diamonds Winery 10, 31, 68, 74
Astro, The 18, 28
Atelier Fine Foods 31
Auberge du Soleil 18
Autocamp Russian River 18
Bardessono 18
Bardos Cider 16
Barrett, Heidi 41
Basque Boulangerie Café 25
Bay Area Rodeo 22
Bear Flag Monument 8, 25
Bear Flag Revolt 39, 63
Beaulieu Vineyard 45, 63, 64 93, 97
Beckstoffer, Andy 47
Benson, Jeremy 21
Big Ranch Farms 20
Birds, The 57
Bistro Jeanty 17
Bodega Dunes 19

Bodega Head Trail 11
Bodkin Wines 96
Bohemia Ecological Preserve 9
Bohemian Grove 78, 22, 43
Bohemian Highway [*company*] 8
Bohemian Highway [*route*] 11
Bonné, Jon 12
Bookmine 20
Boon Hotel + Spa 18
Bothe-Napa Valley State Park 11
BottleRock 8
Bottling 65
Bouchon Bistro 28
Boyle, T. Coraghessan 12
Bromige, David 41
Brot 17
Brown Estate 68, 96
Brown, Alexandria 89
Buena Vista Vineyard 45, 69
Bufano, Beniamino 35
Burbank, Luther 42
Butter & Egg Days 22
Butter Cream Bakery 17
Cafe San Marco 27
California Artisan Cheese Festival 22
California Indian Museum and Cultural Center 10

Calistoga Motor Lodge + Spa 18
Cameo Cinema 27
Cameron, Frank 56
Cannetti Roadhouse 34
Carneros clay 64
Carneros Region 32
Carneros Resort 32
Carpenter, Tina 21
Carter & Co. 21
Cartograph Wines 26
Ceja Vineyards 69
Charles Krug Winery 8, 27, 63
Chateau Montelena Winery 45, 93
Chavez, Cesar 48
Checkerboard Vineyards 53
Cheese 9
CIA at Copia 20
Ciccio 31
Cline, Emma 12
Coastal prairie 9
Cobb Wines 69
Codrescu, Andrei 42, 63
Cody, Morrill 56
Comora, Lu 21
Compline 17, 25
Conaway, James 12
Connaughton, Kyle 80
Contimo Provisions 16
Copperfield's Books 20

Coppola, Francis Ford 54
Corison Winery 68
Coturri Winery 82
Coturri, Tony 82
Cramps, The 12
Crane Park 19
Crooked Goat Brewing 29
Custom Costumes 29
Daniel, John 54
Dehlinger Winery 69
Del Dotto's Vineyards 27
DeLoach Vineayrds 34
Di Rosa Center for Contemporary Art 32
Dierk's Parkside Café 17
Diggers, The 46
Dirty & Rowdy Family Winery 67
Donelan Family Wines 69
Drinkward Peschon 68
Drop City 12
Dry Creek General Store 20
Eagle Cycling Club 31
East Ridge Trail 19
Ehret, Terry 41
El Bonita Motel 18
El Coqui 17
El Molino Central 16
Élevage 65
Elyse Winery 31
Embrace Calistoga 18

Enfield Wine Co 69
Erickson Fine Art 26
Erin Martin 20
Etude 45
Expanding Universe, The 35
Falcon Crest 46
Family farms 13
Far Niente Winery 45
Farmer's Wife 29
Farmstead 17
Fatted Calf, The 17
Fermentation 65
Fernandez, Olga 70
Festa Italiana 22
Film 12
Florence Avenue 29
Fogbelt Brewing 28
Foote Botanical Preserve 9
Fort Ross 62, 63
Francis Ford Coppola Winery 10
French Laundry, The 16, 31, 50
Frog's Leap 68
Furniture Marolles 21
Gaiter, Dorothy J. 92
Gallery Lulo 20
Gallo, Ernest and Julio 33
Genova Delicatessen 16
Girard Winery 28
Girls & the Fig 16
Girls, The 12
Glass Fire 63
Godseye 21

Gold Coast Bakery 35
Goldman, Anne 103
Goldridge Series 64
Gottlieb, Lou 46
Gotts 25
Grape harvesting and sorting 65
Grape pressing 65
Green Door, The 16
Green Valley AVA 34
Grgich, Mike 45
Grider, John 48
Guerneville 26
Guerneville Pride Parade 26
Guerneville Taco Truck 16
Guerrero Fernandez Winery 70
Gundlach Bundschu Winery 10, 32, 67
Hagafen Cellars 96
Hall Wines 27
Hand Fan Museum 26
Haraszthy, Agoston 41, 45, 56, 59, 63
Harold Richardson Redwoods Reserve 19
Harvest Moon Estate and Winery 34
Healdsburg 26
Healdsburg Jazz Festival 26
Healdsburg Running Company 19
Hedren, Tippi 57
Heitz Cellar 68, 96

Hellenthal
  Vineyard 77
Hellenthal, Elisa 77
Hernandez,
  Madeline 23
Hess Collection 10
Hideaway 29
Hirsch Vineyards
  10, 26, 69
Hitchcock, Alfred 57
Hook & Ladder
  Winery 34
Horse & Plow
  Cider 29
Hotel La Rose 18
Hotel Petaluma 29
House of Mondavi,
  The 12
Housing 13
Hudson Ranch 32
Hudson Ranch &
  Vineyards 32
Huerta, Dolores 48
Huether, Gordon 23
Huichica music
  festival 22
Huichica Series 64
Ide, William 39
Indian Springs 18, 27
Inglenook 45, 54, 58
Iron Horse
  Vineyards 34
Italian Swiss
  Colony 45
Jessup Cellars 28
John Barleycorn 59
Johnson, Denis 12
Johnson's Beach 26
Jolie-Laide 67
Joseph Phelps

Vineyards 67
KBBF 89.1 8
Keller, Thomas 16, 17
Kelly, Mikey 21
Kendall-Jackson 45
Khaledi, Kashy 74
King, Gail 42
Koch, William I. 40
Krug, Charles 41, 63
Kurniawan, Rudy 40
L'Objet Wines 96
La Luna Market
  and Taqueria 27
La Sirena 53
Lail, Robin 54
Larkmead
  Vineyards 33, 96
Layland, David 23
Lazy Bear
  Weekend 26
Lighted Tractor
  Parade 27
Limeliters, The 12
London, Jack 59
Lou's
  Luncheonette 32
Luedtke, Christa 17
Luning, David 12
Luther Burbank
  Experimental
  Farm 42
Macriado, El 48
Mad Fritz 17
Malolactic fermen
  tation [MLF] 65, 66
Marcassin
  Vineyard 53
Mariani, Andrew 86
Marine soils 64
Martha Stoumen

Wines 69
Martin, Dean 45
Martini, Louis 41
Massican Winery 68
Matthiasson
  Winery 68
McClellan,
  Martha 41
McDaniel,
  Richard 21
McDonough,
  Elise 23
Mercadito 16
Meshulam,
  Phyllis 21
Mi Sueño 96
Microclimates 62
Millennials 13
Miller, Jeffrey 42
Miminashi 17
Mission grapes 63
Mobley, Esther 23
Model Bakery 17
Mondavi family 51
Mondavi, Marc 23
Mondavi, Robert 51
Monte Rio Variety
  Show 22
Moore Creek Park 27
Morning Star
  Ranch 46
Mount Veeder
  Winery 66
Murphy's Irish
  Pub 25
Music 12
Mustards Grill 16
Napa [*town*] 25
Napa Bay River
  Trail 9

Napa Farmers Market 25
Napa Makes 22
Napa River Velo 8
Napa Soda Springs 5
Napa Solano Ridge Trail 11
Napa Valley 1839 FC 22
Napa Valley Aloft 19
Napa Valley Bike Tours 31
Napa Valley Museum 28
Napa Valley Paddle 19
Napa Valley Vine Trail 31
Napa: The Story of an American Eden 12
Naysayer Coffee 25
New California Wine, The 12
Nichelini Family Winery 10
Niebaum, Gustave 54
Nolan, Pat 41
Northern Light Surf Shop 19
Oak woodland 9
Oat Hill Mine 19
Odette Estate Winery 68
Old Faithful Geyser of California 9
Old Main Street Saloon 17, 29
Olive oil 9
Olivet Road 34
Olmo, Harold 33, 38

Opera House Collective 20
Outland 10, 25
Pancha's 28
Parker, Robert 58
Passalaqua, Tegan 41
Pat's International 26
Peay Vineyards 69
Petaluma 29
Petroski, Dan 33
Phylloxera 40, 62, 63
Plank Coffee 26
Pleshette, Suzanne 57
Poe Wines 70
Pomace shovel 65
Pomo Canyon Environmental Campground 35
Porchfest 22
Priest Ranch 28
Primary notes and aromas 66
Prohibition 52
Public transit 8
Pygmy forest 9
Rainbow Cattle Company 26
Readers' Books 20, 25
Rebuild NorthBay 23
Reeve Wines 69
Reichl, Ruth 50
Ridge Vineyards 10, 69
Rivertown Revival 29
Robert Louis Stevenson 10
Robert Mondavi Winery 45, 54, 63, 92
Robert Sinskey Vineyards 68
Roche + Roche 23

Roy's 29
Russian colonialism 53
Russian River poets 42
Rutherford Bench 64
Sage Canyon Road 11
Salt Point State Park 9
San Andreas Fault 62, 64
San Antonio altar wine 45
Sando, Steve 76
Santa Rosa 28
Santa Rosa Press Democrat 8
Santa Rosa Rural Cemetery 11
Sarris, Greg 98
Schoener, Abe 70
Schoonmaker, Frank 108
Schramsberg Vineyards 10, 63
Scout West County 20
Screaming Eagle 45
Scribe Winery 10, 32, 69, 86
Sea Ranch, The 49
Sebastopol 29
Second Chances 29
Seghesio Family Vineyards 69
Seguin Moreau 21
Shabram, Patrick 64
Shackford's 20
Shaffer-Killey, Shannon 81

Sheehan, Samantha 70
Sherlock Holmes 63
Shipwright & Co. 21
Siler, Julia Flynn 12
Silverado Squatters, The 52
SingleThread 18, 80
Sky Vineyards 68
Solari, Larry 33
Somerston Estate 28
Sones, Jacqueline 23
Sonoma [*town*] 25
Sonoma International Film Festival 22
Sonoma Valley Authors Festival 22
Soter, Tony 45
Southern Pomo 47
Spinster Sisters, The 28
Spy 42
St Clair Brown Winery 31
St Helena 27
St Helena Star 38, 51
Stags' Leap Winery 53, 66
Starling 25
Station Coffee 27
Stauffacher, Barbara 49
Steinbeck Series 64
Sterling, Joy 34
Steve's Hardware 20
Stevenson, Robert Louis 52
Stewart Cellars 28
Stony Hill Vineyard 10
Summer water 45
Suscol Intertribal Powwow 22
Tacos Chavez 16
Tacos Garcia 28
Tank Garage Winery 27
Taylor Lane Organic Coffee 29
Tchelistcheff, André 41
Tertiary notes and aromas 66
The Terraces 67
Timber Cove 18, 35
Ting Hau 28
To-Kalon Vineyard 47
Tra Vigne Pizzeria 17
Trancas Steakhouse 25
Treehorn Books 20
Trefethen Family Vineyards 31
Trione-Annadel State Park 9
Triple Creek Horse Outfit 19
Tsu, Cecilia 23
Tulocay Cemetary 25
Turley Wine Cellars 68
Turley, Helen 41
Two-Buck Chuck 45
University of California, Davis 58
Valdez Family Winery 70
Valdez, Elizabeth 70
Valencia, Arleene Correa 85
Vallejo, Mariano 41
Villa Ca'Toga 27
Vision Cellars 96
Voelcker, Hunce 41
Volcanic soils 64
Volpi's 17
Waits, Tom 12
Walker, Neil Alexander 23
Ware, Marianne 41
Washoe House 29, 45
Weinberger, Andy 25
Weinberger, Hannah 49, 63
Western Farm Center 20
Westside Road 11
Wild mustard 25
Wildfires 5, 13
Wine bottles of note 67
Wine climate 62
Wine geology 62
Wine history 62
Wine tasting 66
Wine thief 65
Winegrowing soil varieties 64
Winemaking production cycle 65
Winiarski, Warren 41, 96
Wiser, Leslie 79
Wolf, Kate 12
Wonton soup, California's best 28
Yountville 28, 31
Zellerbach, James 56